Robert Mugabe and
the Betrayal of Zimbabwe

Robert Mugabe and the Betrayal of Zimbabwe

by ANDREW NORMAN

McFarland & Company, Inc., Publishers

Jefferson, North Carolina, and London

Also by Andrew Norman

HMS Hood: Pride of the Royal Navy (2001)
By Swords Divided: Corfe Castle in the Civil War (2003)
T. E. Lawrence: Unravelling the Enigma (2003)
Tyneham: The Lost Village of Dorset (2003)

LIBRARY OF CONGRESS CATALOGUING-IN-PUBLICATION DATA

Norman, Andrew, 1943–
    Robert Mugabe and the betrayal of Zimbabwe / by Andrew Norman.
        p.   cm.
    Includes bibliographical references and index.

    ISBN 0-7864-1686-6 (softcover : 50# alkaline paper) ∞

    1. Mugabe, Robert Gabriel, 1924–   2. Presidents—Zimbabwe—Biography.   3. Zimbabwe—Politics and government—1980–   I. Title.
DT3000.M28N67 2004
968.9105'1'092—dc22

                                        2003028285

British Library cataloguing data are available

Cover images ©2004 Art Today

Manufactured in the United States of America

McFarland & Company, Inc., Publishers
   Box 611, Jefferson, North Carolina 28640
      www.mcfarlandpub.com

To the long-suffering people of Zimbabwe,
of whatever race or creed.

Oftentimes, to win us to our harm,
The instruments of darkness tell us truths;
Win us with honest trifles, to betray's
In deepest consequence.

—Shakespeare, *Macbeth*

Acknowledgments

My thanks to the Rt. Hon. The Baroness Thatcher; the Movement for Democratic Change in Harare, Zimbabwe; the South African High Commission in London; Macmillan Publishers Ltd. in London; and the Rt. Hon. Peter Hain.

Thanks also to Jean and Jane Norman for reminiscences and the loan of photographs. Thanks also to Vivyan Tothill for providing her father Charles Blankenburg's account of the Jameson Raid; to Lynette Hodges for the loan of photographs and for showing me "My Memories" by her great-grandmother, Julie Harris; also to the Pitt Rivers Museum in Oxford for information about the Zimbabwe birds.

Especial thanks go to the *Observer* for kind provision of photographs.

And to Tom Gillibrand, Jon Moy-Thomas, Robert Doe, Peter Devlin, Brigid Chapman, Thomas Norman, Rod Cox, Michael Dragffy, the staff of Poole and Canford Cliffs libraries, and especially to Rachel Dragffy for all help and encouragement.

Contents

Contents

Preface

Robert Gabriel Mugabe was born in 1924. The son of a humble carpenter at a Jesuit mission, he rose to become president of his country: Zimbabwe (formerly Southern Rhodesia).

Zimbabwe is a country of 50,000 square miles—virtually the same size as England—with a population of 10.5 million, of whom 77 percent are Shona, 17 percent Ndebele, and 1.4 percent European. Landlocked, and situated within the tropics, it is bordered by the Zambezi River to the north and the Limpopo to the south. Its neighbors are Zambia (to the north), Mozambique (to the east), South Africa (to the south), and Botswana and Namibia (to the west).

The capital is Harare (formerly Salisbury), with a population of 1.2 million. Other major cities are Bulawayo (in Matabeleland) and Gweru (formerly Gwelo). Topographical features include game reserves, the mountainous eastern districts, Victoria Falls, and Kariba—once the largest manmade lake in the world. Zimbabwe's central plateau (or high veld) is between 1,200 and 1,500 meters above sea level, and for this reason the temperature in summer seldom rises above 35 degrees C, and in winter seldom falls below 5 degrees C. The annual rainfall of between 300 mm and 1,000 mm falls between November and March, after which it is normal to have eight or nine months of total drought.

My interest in Mugabe, who became prime minister of Zimbabwe

13

The author with his parents, circa 1957.

in 1980 and has been president since 1987, arose from the fact that my family and I spent four years in his country in the 1950s; when my sister Jane and I were teenagers and my father and mother ran a government school. Ever since then, the country and its people have held an enduring fascination for me.

We arrived there in 1956, and went to live in the town of Gwelo, where two years previously, Mugabe had worked as a schoolteacher while at the same time he had studied for a degree by correspondence course. By that time, Mugabe was 32 and had already shown early signs of promise and strength of character. He had become a teacher with the encouragement of his mentor, Father O'Hea, at the mission. When his father abandoned his family, Mugabe assumed financial responsibility, not only for his own mother and his five siblings, but also for his father's three children by a second marriage (his father having returned home and subsequently died). Conflict with the white minority government would result in his being imprisoned for ten years. Finally, after a bitter civil war in which he was principal organizer, the Lancaster House Agreement of 1979 brought peace, independence, and black majority rule.

Even when in prison, Mugabe continued to study. He eventually obtained another six university degrees, was awarded several honorary degrees by various countries, served as chairman of many of Africa's most prestigious organizations, and was invested on a 1994 state visit to Britain with the rank of an Honorary Knight Grand Cross of the Most Honourable Order of the Bath by Her Majesty, Queen Elizabeth II.

Those heady days, when the people of the newly named Zimbabwe rightly hoped and expected to reap the rewards of independence and gain control of their own lives and destiny, today seem a distant dream, as this once flourishing country plunges ever deeper into economic ruin. Mugabe, instead of leading his people to the promised land, has on the one hand amassed a fortune for himself, his family and followers, and on the other presided over the deliberate murder, torture, and starvation of those who oppose him. Even the veterans who fought in the struggle for independence are now being dispossessed of their lands. In short, Mugabe has betrayed his people.

In writing this book I have attempted to explain the phenomenon of Mugabe. The present being rooted in the past, it is first necessary to understand where the various people who make up Zimbabwe—Mugabe included—have come from in terms of the historic migration of peoples to that land over the centuries: blacks from the north, whites from the south. It is also necessary to see Mugabe in the context of the ideas that predominated at various stages of the country's history, such as the missionary era as personified by David Livingstone; the colonialist era as epitomized by Cecil Rhodes; and the present post–Harold Macmillan "wind of change" era of independence from colonial rule.

How did an insignificant boy, the son of a deeply devout Catholic mother—a boy who continued with his studies no matter what the circumstances, who looked after his family in its time of crisis, and who embraces cricket as a game played by gentlemen—become an autocratic and ruthless tyrant who rigs elections, tramples over the rule of law, and exhibits blatant racism against the mainly Shona opposition party (the Movement for Democratic Change) as well as against the whites and especially against the white farmers?

What are the influences of his first and second wife, and of his long years of imprisonment, on his character and behavior? Is he motivated simply by greed, or do other factors play a disproportionate part in his thinking and reasoning?

In my research I have made use of material that I gleaned from Zimbabwe in the 1950s; articles from newspapers, both Zimbabwean and British; television news bulletins and documentaries on Zimbabwe; Internet websites including those of the Zimbabwean government and the MDC; the Lancaster House Agreement; historical documents such as Julie Harris's diary; and current books on the subject.

1

Origins of Southern Rhodesia

In the Matopos hills, situated near Bulawayo, are granite caves on the walls of which are paintings depicting humans and animals—buck, giraffe, zebra, elephant—in monochromatic colors of red, yellow, black and white. In other caves of the same era are depicted fishes and snakes. These images were created by the so-called Bushmen, who were the native inhabitants of the land.

Bushmen are small in stature, with a wrinkled appearance to their skin, excellent eyesight, and a fondness for art and song. Caves were their preferred habitat but they also lived in primitive huts made of branches. Their skill as trackers is legendary. The European settlers and missionaries who arrived on the continent were unable to understand the language of the Bushmen, which abounds with "clicking" noises. (The Xhosa people of today, who are related to the Zulus, also use clicking sounds in their language.)

The new settlers were unable to befriend the Bushmen or to work with them. Because of this lack of communication, the Bushmen, now regarded as aliens in their own land, were hunted down and virtually exterminated. There were said to be none remaining in Rhodesia and fewer than 1,000–2,000 in southwest Africa. If the Bushmen were the original inhabitants of Rhodesia and none now

An African village—a *kraal*.

remain in the country, where did Zimbabwe's present black population originate from?

"Bantu" refers to a people deriving originally from the Niger/ Congo region who, having learned to cultivate crops and use metals to make tools, dispersed themselves over the course of about 2,000 years across the whole of sub-equatorial Africa.[1] By the tenth century, if not before, the Karangas—Shona-speaking descendents of the Bantu—had colonized present-day Rhodesia and Nyasaland together with the lowlands of Mozambique and had made their capital at Zimbabwe, 200 miles south of what would later be called Salisbury. Here they discovered and learned to work gold, copper and tin, and built their royal palace of Zimbabwe (attributed by carbon dating to approximately the eleventh century),[2] one of 300 or so stone-built edifices constructed by the Karangas over the next four centuries. Gold and ivory were transported eastward, to the port of Sofala in Mozambique, where they were shipped by Arab traders using dhows to Oman and, from there, to China and India.[3] Other Karanga people traveled south and colonized the region between the Limpopo and Vaal Rivers—later known as the Transvaal—or crossed the Vaal into what later became the "Orange Free State."

By the mid-fifteenth century, the Rotsi, a Shona-Speaking people from the south, became predominant in the region; they took over the royal palace of Zimbabwe and the valuable mines. However, early in the sixteenth century, the Portuguese, in an attempt to gain control of the gold and ivory trade from the interior, colonized Mozambique and captured Sofala, thus replacing the Arabs as trading partners of the Rotsis. Minerals and slaves were traded, and along the slave-caravan routes were huge holding pits, dug out of the ground and surrounded by high stone walls with locked gates, where the unfortunate slaves were kept manacled together overnight until the following day's march from the interior toward the coast.

Therefore, unlike the Bushmen, the Bantu were not indigenous to Rhodesia and southern Africa: despite the fact that the Southern Rhodesian whites invariably referred to them as "natives." Where then did European immigrants arrive from?

Colonization of the Cape of Good Hope by the Dutch began in earnest with the Dutch East India Company's establishment of a charter, granted in the Hague on March 20, 1602. The first Dutchman to colonize the Cape of Good Hope was the surgeon Jan Van Riebeek, who was born in Holland in 1618. However, when the first Dutch colonists settled in the Cape in 1652, the Bantu had already established themselves near the Fish River, which was located 500 miles to the east of Cape Town.[4]

Dutch persisted as the written and cultural language for the settlers until the nineteenth century; they then developed their own language—Afrikaans—which evolved during the 150-year occupation of the Cape by the Dutch East India Company. In 1918, Afrikaans was made the official language of the Union of South Africa, and in 1925 it became the official language of Parliament.

From where did the British presence in Southern Rhodesia originate, and how did the country get its name? The British seized the

Cecil John Rhodes (© the Rhodes Trust)

Cape of Good Hope during the Napoleonic Wars of the late eighteenth and early nineteenth centuries in order to prevent the French from claiming it; the first British settlers arrived in 1806. Their presence, however, did not please the Afrikaners—or Boers, as they were also called.

In 1833 the British House of Commons passed a law that forbade slavery throughout the dominions of King William IV. At that time, there were in excess of 30,000 slaves in the Cape Colony, whom the farmers (mainly Boers) depended on for their economic survival. Compensation was offered but was deemed inadequate and this, together with a dislike of bureaucracy and taxation, was the main reason for the Boer migration northwards in the "Great Trek"—those who participated were the "Voortrekkers." During this trek, the Voortrekkers had many bloody battles with the Zulus.

The Boers subsequently established the Republic of Natalia and, when the British asserted their authority there also, further treks were eventually made into what became the Transvaal and the Orange Free State. In 1843 these two areas were declared Independent Boer Republics, and Natal was declared a British colony.

Rhodesia was named after Cecil John Rhodes, who was born at Bishop's Stortford in Hertfordshire, England, on July 5, 1853. At 17, Rhodes, who suffered from tuberculosis of the lungs, was sent to Natal—where his brother was already an established farmer—so that the clean air would improve his health, which it did. When diamonds were discovered at Kimberley in the Orange Free State, Rhodes moved there and set up a prosperous business, selling excavating equipment and water pumps for the newly opened mines. This led, in 1880, to his founding of the De Beers Diamond Mining Company. Rhodes was also active in politics and was appointed to the Cabinet of the Cape Colony in 1884 (for a brief time, he was its treasurer). When gold was discovered on the Rand (Witwatersrand, an area to the south of Johannesburg in the Transvaal), Rhodes invested in those fields and, in 1887, established the Goldfields of South Africa Company.

In 1888 Rhodes, ever ambitious, sent Charles Rudd, his business partner at Kimberley, and two others north to the country soon to bear his name: Southern Rhodesia. Here they met with Lobengula, king of the Matabele, at his capital Gubulawayo, ("the place of the killing," later known as Bulawayo), situated just to the north of the Matopos Hills. Two years earlier, following a visit from Scottish missionary the Reverend J.S. Moffat of Bechuanaland, brother-in-law of David Livingstone, Lobengula had entered into a treaty, giving certain rights to the British authorities.

Lobengula was not originally of royal blood. His father, Mosele-

21

katse, had been a general in the army of the great Zulu chief, Tshaka, of present-day Natal. Following a dispute with Tshaka, Moselekatse fled north in 1834 and crossed the Limpopo River. His Zulus devastated the region, forcing the Rotsi (Shona) inhabitants to retreat westward, and Moselekatse and his followers settled principally in the area of the Matopos Hills, his people being known as the "Matabele" ("those who disappear," or, in other words, those who can blend in easily with the bush). Finally, the territory was divided, with the Shona, who became subjects of the Matabele, occupying the north and east (Mashonaland); the Matabele, the south and west (Matabeleland). (The "Moselekatse Roller," named after the great Zulu king, is a beautiful bird about the size of a blackbird with blue and lilac plumage. Tradition holds that no one except the current Zulu monarch may use its feathers for decoration.)

Rhodes' partner Charles Rudd offered 1,000 rifles, 10,000 bullets, a steamboat with guns for use on the Zambesi, and £1,200 a year to Lobengula and his heirs, in return for which Lobengula signed away the mineral rights to his "kingdom, principalities and dominions." The document was sent back to Rhodes in South Africa who, having presented it to the British government, was a year later granted a Royal Charter for his British South Africa Company (BSAC).

Rhodes' problems were still not over because Edward Lippert, a German Jew, had already obtained mineral concessions in Matabeleland from Lobengula, which were of such high value that Rhodes was obliged to negotiate with Lippert in order to exploit his own mining interests in that place. This resulted in the Lippert Concession (1889), which allowed would-be British settlers to acquire land rights from the indigenous people.[5] In practice, the BSAC bought concessions from the British Crown and then sold them to the settlers, the revenue accruing to the Crown, and the owners of the land receiving nothing.

Rhodes now contracted 23-year-old Major Frank Johnson—formerly of the Bechuanaland Border Police—to organize a Pioneer Column that would occupy Mashonaland.[6] The Column, consisting of 200 hired adventurers (none of them over the age of 25) and guided by the famous elephant hunter Frederick Courteney Selous, set off from Macloutsie in the British Protectorate of Bechuanaland on

June 28, 1890. On July 11, the Column crossed the River Tuli to begin its 400-mile trek into Mashonaland. This day was known thereafter as Rhodes and Founders Day, which all Rhodesian schoolchildren have since celebrated as a holiday. Eleven weeks later, a makeshift road was built, which miners and farmers would follow: the Union flag was raised to a 21-gun salute on a hill near Mount Hampden in Mashonaland, which became known first as Fort Salisbury and later simply as Salisbury.

There was one problem. The fabled gold, which German geologist Karl Mauch (who had inspired the whole enterprise) said he had discovered there, was nowhere to be found. This caused many of the Pioneers, who had each been promised a farm and 15 gold claims, to give up in disgust and return to Johannesburg; shares in the BSAC plummeted from £3 15s to 12s.[7] However, others remained and became the first white settlers to colonize Mashonaland.

Since the "gold rush" was a disappointment, the Pioneers turned their attention to the land and claimed the 3,175-acre farms promised to them by Cecil Rhodes. Those who followed the pioneers did even better. Leander Starr Jameson, the BSAC's administrator and a medical doctor, encouraged the settlers to claim as many acres as they wanted, irrespective of the blacks who were living on the land at the time. Rhodes' aides were extremely well rewarded. For example, Major Sir John Willoughby, the Column's chief-of-staff, founded a company that eventually acquired 1.3 million acres. Missionaries also benefited, to the tune of one-third of one million acres. Within ten years, one-sixth of the land of Rhodesia—totaling about 16 million acres—had been seized by whites.

The Matabele had been in the habit of extracting tribute from their subject people, the Mashonas. But with a European presence in Mashonaland, tensions grew and came to a head when the Matabele attacked Mashona *kraals* near Fort Victoria, killing the inhabitants and looting their possessions. When Dr. Jameson, the BSAC administrator, ordered the Matabele *impis* to vacate the area and they refused, war was inevitable.

Realizing the weakness of his position, Dr. Jameson organized three attacking columns: one under the command of Major Patrick Forbes in Salisbury; the second under Major Alan Wilson at Fort

Victoria; and the third under Colonel Goold Adams and Commandant Pieter Raaf in Bechuanaland. Various attacks by the Matabele were repulsed with the use of Maxim machine guns, and, on November 4, 1893, the first two columns marched side by side to King Lobengula's headquarters, where all they found was the burning remains of the royal *kraal* (village) and two abandoned Europeans whose lives had been spared by the king's command. Lobengula, with his remaining *impis*, had apparently fled towards the Zambezi River.

Dr. Jameson knew there would be no peace while Lobengula remained at large, and he therefore ordered Major Forbes (who had wrested the area around Umtali known as Manicaland from the Portuguese three years before) and his column to set off in pursuit. At Forbes' side, mounted on a great cream-colored charger, rode Major Allan Wilson. They traveled northward, first to the mission at Inyati and then to the Bubi River, where they decided to turn back. Had they gone on, they might have captured Lobengula, who was a mere three miles further on, with only a handful of warriors to protect him.[8]

The column returned to Inyati, then progressed to the deserted mission station at Shiloh where, as the first heavy rains of the season fell, fresh supplies were obtained. Forbes set off again in pursuit; but after four days, finding his forces to be too slow and unwieldy, he sent his supply wagons and half his men back. This left 160 men, mounted on the best horses.

The pursuit continued across the Bembesi River, then the Bubi, the Gwampa and the Lupani. Now the column had to contend not only with heavy rains, but with a terrain densely covered with mopani trees and thorn bushes. However, each day, scouts sent ahead informed Forbes that he was gaining on the enemy.

Suddenly, two of Forbes' troopers were met by two emissaries of King Lobengula, who offered them a bag of gold and a message of peace. However, the troopers kept the gold for themselves and failed to report the matter to their superiors. On December 3rd, Forbes' column was so close that it came upon the king's last camp—with the cooking fire still burning.

Sensing that there was no time to waste, Forbes then sent Allan Wilson ahead with Captains Judd, Kirton, Greenfield, and Napier and with three scouts and twelve men to continue the pursuit. With the help of a black guide, this patrol discovered several Matabele encampments—visible by the lights of their cooking fires—to which Captain Napier called out in their own language, Sindebele, that he wished to speak to the king. When at last they came to a fenced encampment, Major Wilson knew that they had achieved their objective.

They yelled for Lobengula to surrender but no answer came. Realizing that they had grossly underestimated the strength of the Matabele, Wilson ordered Captain Napier, Scout Mayne and Trooper Robertson to return to Forbes and acquaint him with the position, but by the time they reached Forbes it was almost midnight. Since it would be suicidal to move in the hours of darkness, Forbes decided to send Captain Borrow with 20 men as a reinforcement, but to wait with his main party until daybreak. At 2 A.M., Borrow reached Wilson, and they decided to turn in for the night.

The rain continued to fall steadily. Scout Burnham had no coat, but when he awoke from sleep he found that the unselfish Allan Wilson had covered him with his own cape and had sat up himself to keep watch. Even though virtually cut off, and hopelessly outnumbered, Wilson made the decision to mount a dawn attack. When this failed, Scouts Burnham and Ingram and Trooper Gooding—who had the best horses—were sent back to inform Forbes of the resistance. However, when they did so, they found Forbes' main force was itself under attack from other Matabele.

Wilson and his men were then attacked by a force of about 2,000 warriors, including the elite regiments of Imbezu and Ingubu. Forbes' party, who were stranded on the other side of the Shangani River, could only stand by with frustration as they heard the sounds of gunfire and the bloodcurdling shrieks of the Matabele as Allan Wilson's men fought to the last. It was December 4, 1893. Afterwards, an old *induna* (tribal leader) who had been present at the fight paid the British a final tribute: "These were men," he said.[9]

In the Matopos Hills is an austere, oblong monument to Major Allan Wilson and his column and their defeat on the banks of the Shangani River. Designed by John Tweed, and dedicated by Bishop Gaul of Mashonaland in 1904, the monument is 33 feet high and made of granite blocks hewn from a neighboring kopje. A panel on each of its four sides depicts the members of the patrol in bas relief. It was erected at the express request of Cecil Rhodes.

The white settlers built a shantytown on the site of Lobengula's royal *kraal*. Originally referred to as the "Old Camp," it was later named as Gubulawayo (ominously, "the place of the killing"), and later on simply as Bulawayo. It was there that Rhodes built himself an official residence.

When the monthlong Matabele War ended with the occupation of Bulawayo, Matabele cattle were shared out among the settlers. Two years later, the country was officially named Rhodesia, after Cecil Rhodes. For three years Rhodes had been prime minister of the Cape Colony, but in 1896 he was to make a gross error of judgment. With the discovery of gold in the Transvaal, people of many nations had flocked there in the hope of making their fortunes, but they were not welcomed by the Boers under their president, Paulus Kruger, who referred to them as "Uitlanders" (immigrants).

Recognizing the grievances of the Uitlanders, and hoping to unseat President Kruger, Rhodes now lent his support to an invasion of the Transvaal—to be led by his close friend, Dr. Leander Starr Jameson. However, the Jameson Raid of January 1896 was a failure. Its leaders were imprisoned by the Boers, though treated humanely and later released, and Dr. Jameson was sent back to England where he was tried and sentenced to 15 months' imprisonment. As a result of this disastrous enterprise, Rhodes was forced to retire both as prime minister of the Cape Colony and as managing director of the BSAC.

The defeat of Dr. Jameson by the Boers made the Matabele realize that the European forces were not invincible, and in March 1896 they rose in rebellion, murdering an estimated one-tenth of the white population in an orgy of violence in which the Mashonas were not slow to join in. The terrified inhabitants of Salisbury, Bulawayo and other centers then formed *laagers*, a tactic used by the Voortrekkers, whereby wagons were drawn into a circle and the spaces in between sealed off with thornbushes. The men defended the children and cattle, who remained within the safety of the circle, while the women loaded the guns and treated the wounded.[10]

Subduing the fearsome Matabele warriors, who were expert in the use of the short, stabbing *assegai*, was no easy task: even after

Colonel Plumer arrived in Southern Rhodesia with reinforcements from the Cape. However, Cecil Rhodes brought the Matabele Rebellion to an end when, accompanied by three Europeans and two blacks, he walked unarmed into the Matabele stronghold in the Matopos Hills for an *indaba* (discussion) and persuaded the *indunas* to lay down their arms. In Mashonaland the rebellion dragged on for another year; the fighting finally ended in October 1897.

The Native Reserves Order in Council of 1898 created reserves designated for blacks only on land that was of low quality, at a time when whites were appropriating the most fertile land for themselves.[11] For the whites, a legislative assembly was established and Rhodes promised that, eventually, they would be granted self-government.[12] Also in 1898 the railway was extended from Vryburg and Mafeking (in the northern Cape) to Bulawayo, and, by 1899, the line from the port of Beira (in Mozambique) had reached Umtali and Salisbury.

By 1898 Rhodes, although severely criticized for his support of the abortive Jameson Raid, had resumed his position as managing director of BSAC. Now the South African (or Boer) War would pit one European power against another. At its outbreak in 1899, Rhodes was at Kimberley, where he remained throughout its 124-day siege by the Boers.

The first Boer War of 1880 arose with an attempt by the Boers of the Transvaal to rise up and assert their independence. This culminated with a defeat for the British at Majuba (the "Hill of Doves"), near Charlestown, on the border with Natal. After the failure of the Jameson Raid in 1896, further fighting began in October 1899, marking the beginning of the second Boer War.

The Boers from their Republics of Transvaal and the Orange Free State invaded Natal and Bechuanaland and met with great success. In the so-called Black Week, between December 10 and 15, 1899, Britain suffered three major defeats at Stormberg, Magersfontein, and Colenso. Boer penetration deep into the Cape Province then enabled them to besiege Kimberley, and also Mafeking in Bechuanaland.

General Sir Redvers Buller was then replaced by Lord Roberts as commander in chief of British forces, with Lord Kitchener as his Chief of Staff. Having been considerably reinforced, Roberts, on February 7, 1900, transformed the situation by bringing about the surrender of the Boer general, Piet Cronje, at Paardeberg, thirty miles east of Kimberley on the Modder River. A fortnight later, Bloem-fontein, capital of the Orange Free State, was taken. On May 27 the British crossed the River Vaal at Vereeninging and captured Pretoria, the capital of the Transvaal, on June 5.

However, the Boers under their supreme commander, General Louis Botha, refused to surrender and a guerrilla war began in which they at first achieved some success. In 1900, Kitchener replaced Roberts as commander in chief. His tactics were systematically to cordon off vast tracts of land in order to drive the Boer guerrillas into a corner, whilst at the same time interning tens of thousands of Boer women and children in concentration camps. By separating the men from their homes and families, it was hoped that the Boer guerrillas would lose heart and give in.

Were these camps simply places of internment, or was unneces-sary brutality shown? Some Afrikaners did believe there had been widespread mistreatment, that prisoners were forced to eat sugar with ground glass mixed into it. There beliefs created a definite anti–British bias within Afrikaners. There may well have been isolated incidents of abuse by the British, but the idea of systematic maltreatment on a large scale, or even of genocide such as had occurred in World War II under the Nazis, seems unlikely. Had it occurred, it would undoubt-edly have been reported, since the camps were opened by the British to inspection.

Queen Victoria died on January 22, 1901, and on March 26, 1902, Rhodes himself gave up the long struggle against ill health and died at Muizenburg in the Cape. After lying in state at Groote Schuur and at Parliament House in Cape Town, his body was brought by train through the Transvaal to Bulawayo.

A simple inscription, "HERE LIE THE REMAINS OF CECIL JOHN RHODES," marks his grave at World's View (so-called for obvi-ous reasons) in the Matopos Hills. It was his wish that he be buried there, at a place once revered by the Bushmen, by the Karanga peo-ple (whose name for it was Malindidzimu—the "caves of the spirits"), and by his old adversaries, the Matabele.

Rhodes' will designated the Matopos Hills as a public pleasure ground and World's View as a resting place for "those who have deserved well of their country." His Cape Town residence, Groote Schuur, would become the home of future prime ministers of the Union of South Africa. He left the sum of £100,000 to Oriel—his former Oxford college—and established a trust to provide 60 Rhodes scholarships, each of a value of £250 a year and tenable at Oxford University for three years; these scholarships were to be awarded to young men, mostly from English-speaking regions.

On May 31, 1902, the peace treaty that ended the Boer War was signed at Pretoria. British casualties totaled 97,477. Of this number, 5,774 were killed in battle with more than three times that number dying from wounds, accidents or disease. Boer losses were estimated at 6,000 men, not including deaths in the concentration camps, which one would hope were from disease or natural causes and not deliberately inflicted. The Afrikaners had craved independence and self-government, but they had become pawns in a power struggle: victims of the scramble for territory in Africa.

By the turn of the twentieth century, this scramble for Africa by European powers had left Britain as the largest colonizer, in control of a dozen countries including Kenya, Uganda, Tanganyika, Northern and Southern Rhodesia and Nyasaland, in addition to Cape Province and Natal. To Transvaal and the Orange Free State, Britain granted internal self-government on a whites-only franchise.

The railway continued to creep northward, and at sunrise on April 1, 1905, the mighty Zambezi River was spanned just below the Victoria Falls. (It was Rhodes' wish that the line be built so close to the Falls that spray would fall on the carriages.)

By the eve of World War I in 1914, the land was apportioned as follows: blacks, 24 million acres; BSAC, 48 million acres; individual white settlers, 13 million acres; and private companies, 9 million acres. The total black population was 836,000; the total white population, 28,000. So 3 percent of the population was in possession of 75 percent of the economically productive land, while the remaining 97 percent of the population was confined to 23 percent of lower-grade land in scattered native reserves.[13]

In 1914 a commission investigated growing tensions caused by the conflicting interests of the BSAC and the settlers. Before those problems could be addressed, war broke out in Europe, and the mainly

Stay in Your Car and Stay on the Road—Penalty £5 (National Parks Act)

British white Rhodesians took up arms to support their mother country. No less than one-quarter of the total European population of the country was involved, along with one black regiment, in the fight against the Germans in Southwest Africa and Europe.[14]

When the Union of South Africa came into being on May 31, 1910, it was a Bulawayo lawyer, Charles Coghlan, who helped to draw up its Constitution. He received a knighthood for this work. It was Coghlan's ambition that Rhodesia merge with the Union, but when a referendum was held in October 1923—the year of expiry of the BSAC's Charter—the settlers voted 8,774 to 5,999 in support of domestic self-government. Coghlan, despite his views, became the country's first prime minister. However, the 1923 Constitution gave Britain a continuing role in determining policy for the blacks. The British government paid the BSAC 3.75 million pounds in recognition of its 33-year administration of the country, and the BSAC was allowed to keep its commercial and mineral rights.

The 1920s saw the arrival of the first airplane, the "Silver Queen," and the first motorcars. There were no gas stations—gasoline came only in cans—and a drive from Salisbury to Bulawayo involved the opening and shutting of 500 farm gates!

Agriculture and livestock were of prime importance as far as ordinary Rhodesians were concerned; these served as both their source of food and their source of employment. Cattle were ubiquitous and they included the indigenous Mashona, Tuli and Nkone breeds, as well as Hereford, Angus and Sussex breeds from Britain and Charolais, Simmentaler, Freisland and Holstein breeds from Europe. Also abundant were sheep—the indigenous Persian type and also Dorset Horns and Wiltshires from England. Goats, pigs, poultry and bees were also of prime importance.

The most essential food crop was maize; tobacco—both Virginia and Turkish—was immensely important as an export earner. Cotton, groundnuts, soya beans, sorghum, wheat, tea, coffee, and of course fruit and vegetables were also grown in significant amounts.

Asbestos, beryl, chromite, copper, emerald, garnet, gold, graphite, tin and nickel are among the metals and minerals that were mined. At Wankie in the northeast of Southern Rhodesia were huge reserves of coal, and production at its mines, which had been in operation since

1903, was in excess of 4 million tons per year. However, the pride and joy of the area was its magnificent game reserve, which covered an area of 5,000 square miles—five times the size of the English county of Dorset. There were no physical boundaries to the reserve and the animals were free to wander at will. Tourism in those days was very important to the Rhodesian economy.

Game was abundant, especially antelope, of which eland were the largest, and springbok probably the most nimble; but perhaps the most elegant was the sable with its black body, white belly and horns in the shape of a spiral. Herds of two or three hundred were by no means unusual in those days. There were also lion, giraffe, elephant, buffalo, leopard, zebra and warthog. Today, however, because of the widespread famine that has befallen the country, practically all wild creatures of any size have been killed for food by the country's starving population.

Another tourist attraction was the Victoria Falls, one of the natural wonders of the world. Their roar is like the sound of continuous distant thunder and is audible from ten miles away. At a distance of one mile, the very earth itself trembles; on approaching nearer still, the perpetual rainbow that shines above in the mist comes into view.

The first white man to see the falls was the Scottish missionary and explorer David Livingstone on November 16, 1855, and in the following year he named them after his Queen. In Livingstone's wake would come the great empire-builders of the later nineteenth and early twentieth centuries. The Bantu name for the falls is "Mosi-oa-tunya," or "The smoke that thunders." In 1938 a hydroelectric power plant was opened, which supplied the local area including the town of Livingstone, six miles across the border in Northern Rhodesia, with electricity.

At the local cemetery are the graves of 40 or so early white Settlers—men, women, and children, some in their infancy—who had died at the turn of the century, predominantly of blackwater fever, a deadly form of malaria, where the destruction of red cells by the malaria parasite is so great that the urine actually turns black with degraded blood products.

Something, it seems, that will never change despite all Rhodesia's subsequent political and social upheavals, is the marvel of the Zimbabwe Ruins, situated 75 miles south of Gwelo. The name derives from the Shona words "dzimba dza mabwe," meaning "houses of stone."[15] When Southern Rhodesia became independent, its new name Zimbabwe, derived from this place.

The Acropolis is built on the summit of a kopje and appears to be a fortification. In the valley is the so-called Elliptical Temple, which is approximately 80 meters in length. The Temple consists of two conical structures, one large and the other small, and the remains of other buildings which may have been dwelling places, all of dry-stone construction. The whole is surrounded by a wall roughly 9 meters high and up to 4.5 meters thick. Linking the Acropolis and the Elliptical Temple is the Valley of Ruins, a series of deteriorated walls that extend for nearly a mile.[16]

The Zimbabwe Ruins are the most impressive and elaborate of 400 or so ancient stone buildings situated between the Sabi and Limpopo Rivers. The first white man to discover the Ruins is believed to be Carel Trigardt, a Dutch Voortrekker sometime in the 1830s. No burial grounds, skeletons or inscriptions have been found to give a clue as to its creators or to the date when the Ruins were built. However, many gold ornaments have been found there and, most fascinating of all, eight one-meter-high soapstone statuettes of birds, which look similar to eagles.

Seven of the birds came from the Hill Ruin, thought to be the former palace of a sacred ruler; the eighth is from the Lower Homestead near where the king's wives were confined during their pregnancies. Each carved bird is unique, and each has both human and eagle characteristics. One has lips instead of a beak, and all have four or five toes rather than three talons. The bird from the Lower Homestead is sitting, the others standing. Shonas believe the eagle, which embodies the spirits of former leaders, is a messenger that soars up to heaven to intercede with God over such issues as the provision of sufficient rain for the crops. The fact that no such stone eagles have been discovered at any other site suggests that Zimbabwe was preeminent as a sacred place.[17]

In the 1950s, tourists were seen at the Ruins in abundance. Today, they are few and far between.

In 1924 an event was to occur that would eventually bring about enormous repercussions for the country, although no one could have foreseen such effects at the time. This event was the birth of Robert Mugabe.

2

Mugabe's Early Life

Robert Gabriel Mugabe was born on February 21, 1924, at the Katuma Jesuit Mission, 50 miles west of Salisbury in the Zvimba Tribal Trust Land, which was founded by Jean-Baptiste Loubiere during World War I. Robert was the third of six children born to Gabriel Mugabe, the Mission's carpenter, and his wife Bona; both parents were Roman Catholics, Bona especially so. Katuma was an offshoot of the Chishawasha Mission, built on land donated by the BSAC in gratitude to the Jesuits who had accompanied Rhodes' Pioneer Column on its march into Mashonaland. Robert Mugabe was a solitary child whose only friends, in the words of his brother Donato, were his books. Here, at the Mission school, the Mugabe children were well educated, and Robert achieved the level of Standard VI.

In 1934 Father Loubiere died and was replaced by Father O'Hea, who, despite opposition by the white government in Salisbury, championed the cause of black education by adding at his own expense a teacher-training college and a technical college to the existing primary facilities at Katuma. He also built a hospital to serve the 10,000-square-mile Zvimba Native Reserve, where there previously were no medical facilities whatsoever, and now the duties of physician were added to those of priest and teacher. At Katuma the message preached was for equality between the races, as opposed to the discrimination that was practiced throughout the rest of the country. Father O'Hea's native Ireland had experienced similar problems in its fight for independence from Britain.

At about this time, Mugabe's elder brother Raphael died of an enteric infection. Then in 1934, his eldest brother Michael also died of an unknown ailment. Mugabe's father, who had previously fallen out with Father Loubiere, now left the village and settled in Bulawayo, 300 miles away. His family would hear nothing of him for ten years.

Recognizing in Mugabe "an exceptional mind and an exceptional Heart,"[1] Father O'Hea offered him a place at the teacher-training college. He provided Robert with a bursary, as there was no financial support from his absent father. Politics was becoming increasingly important in Mugabe's life, and in attempting to reconcile it with religion, he stated, "It has always been my firm belief that socialism has to be much more Christian than capitalism."[2]

Having qualified as a primary schoolteacher in 1941, Mugabe stayed at Katuma to teach at his former school, supporting his mother and siblings from his salary of £2 per month. Three years later, his father Gabriel returned, now gravely ill and with three more children born to him by another wife. Shortly afterwards Gabriel died, and Mugabe then found himself financially responsible for six children instead of three. In 1945, having gained his diploma in teaching, Mugabe left Katuma to teach at various schools in Southern Rhodesia, including the Dadaya Mission, where he met the Reverend Ndabaningi Sithole, an aspiring politician who was also a teacher.

In 1949, at the age of 25, Mugabe won a scholarship to the all-black University of Fort Hare in South Africa's Cape Province. It was there that students had created the African National Congress (ANC) in 1912; also, Nelson Mandela (later head of the ANC), had been expelled for leading a student strike in 1940. At Fort Hare, described as a hotbed of African nationalism, Mugabe came into contact with Robert Sobukwe (later the head of the Pan-African Congress), Mangosuthu Buthelezi (the South African Zulu leader), the black activist Leopold Takawira, who introduced him to Marxism, and ANC militant Oliver Tambo. At that time there was immense respect among the university community for Mahatma Gandhi, whose campaign of passive resistance had paved the way for Indian independence.

Robert Mugabe (photograph courtesy of *The Observer*).

Having joined the Youth League wing of the ANC, and gained his B.A. degree in history and english literature in 1951, Mugabe returned to Southern Rhodesia where, in his own words, he found himself "completely hostile to the system." For a year he taught at the Driefontein (Roman Catholic) Mission near Umvuna, 50 miles east of Gwelo; then in 1953 he taught at Salisbury South Primary School. In 1954, Mugabe transferred to a school in Gwelo, where he obtained his B.A. degree in education through a correspondence course from the University of South Africa.

It was the year 1953 that the Federation of the two Rhodesias, Northern and Southern, and Nyasaland, came into being. Its chief advocate was Andrew Cohen, assistant undersecretary of the Africa division of the British Colonial Office. He saw the Federation as a viable economic unit and as a buffer to the Afrikaner-administered South Africa, which was perceived to be Anti–British.

The Federation's first prime minister was Godfrey Huggins, the former prime minister of Southern Rhodesia. Former Northern Rhodesian leader, the colorful Roy Welensky, was the Federation's minister of transport. Welensky was a former heavyweight boxing champion of Rhodesia and had also been a bartender, an engine driver, and then a trade union leader before going into politics. In 1956, he succeeded Huggins as prime minister of the Federation. However, there was a major discrepancy between the views of Huggins and Welensky on the one hand and the British Colonial Office on the other because, unlike Cohen, both men envisaged a prolonged time scale—in Welensky's case over a century—before the blacks would be fully enfranchised and ready to participate in government.[3]

Despite the name "Federation," there was some variation in the degree of autonomy allowed to the three provinces. Nyasaland, the least developed country, was ruled as a Crown colony; Northern Rhodesia was governed through the Colonial Office in London although it had its own local assembly and legislative council of elected members; Southern Rhodesia, the most developed country, was self-governing with its prime minister being R. S. Garfield Todd, a New Zealander who had been a Protestant missionary in the Shabani area for some years. However, matters of common concern to all three countries were presided over by the Federal Parliament in Salisbury.

Each country had its own leader in the fight for black enfranchisement. In Southern Rhodesia, black aspirations were embodied by Joshua Nkomo, who was leader of the National Democratic Party (NDP) and was president of the ANC from 1957. In Northern Rhodesia, politician Kenneth Kaunda, founder of the Northern Rhodesian United National Independence Party, was imprisoned in Gwelo in 1955 for possessing prohibited literature. In Nyasaland Dr. Hastings Banda, leader of the Nyasaland/Malawi Congress Party independence movement, worked as a doctor in Britain and on the Gold Coast.

Opposite, top: **Sir Roy Welensky, prime minister of the Federation of Rhodesia and Nyasaland, 1956–1963 (photograph courtesy of** *The Observer***).** *Bottom:* **Joshua Nkomo (photograph courtesy of** *The Observer***).**

In Gwelo, when Mugabe was a teacher there, a British couple, Guy Clutton-Brock and his wife Molly, organized discussion groups for African teachers aimed at promoting the idea of racial conciliation. In Clutton-Brock's remembrance, Mugabe "neither drank nor smoked," and "had an overwhelming thirst for knowledge." In 1955, dissatisfied with his meager remuneration as a teacher, Mugabe took up an appointment at the Chalimbana Training College in Northern Rhodesia (Zambia), where he stayed for three years; in his spare time, he studied for a third degree: a Bachelor of Science from the University of London. Meanwhile changes had occurred in Zimbabwe that were to entrench the white position of power and to place its black people at a permanent disadvantage.

The Land Apportionment Act of 1930 had formalized the division of land between blacks and whites. The white population, then at 50,000, was assigned 49 million acres of the country's most fertile and productive land. The black population of

1.1 million occupied native reserves totaling 29 million acres, and the remaining 19 million acres were either unassigned or conserved as forests and national parks. The Act also stipulated that no black African was entitled to own land in a "white" area. When Sir Godfrey Huggins became prime minister in 1933, he summarized this position: "The Europeans in this country can be likened to an island in a sea of black, with the artisan and the tradesman forming the shores and the professional classes the highlands in the centre. Is the native to be allowed to erode the shores and gradually attack the highlands?" In 1951 the Native Land Husbandry Act placed further restrictions on black landholders. It was hugely unpopular and was abandoned ten years later.

The year 1957 was not a happy one for the prime minister of Southern Rhodesia, Garfield Todd of the United Rhodesia Party. Rumors circulated that he was having talks with black nationalist leaders without the approval of his colleagues, and matters came to a head when most of his cabinet ministers resigned. Power struggles developed among the white hegemony in and around the capital, Salisbury, 150 miles to the northeast; these struggles would eventually destroy the entire fabric of the country.

Gwelo, where Mugabe worked as a teacher in 1954, was not untypical of other Rhodesian towns in its makeup and traditions. It contained elegant, whitewashed buildings with red roofs and verandas. The streets, set out in a grid system common to all Rhodesian towns, were lined with delicate mauve-blossomed jacaranda trees. At the insistence of Dr. Jameson, these streets were made wide enough to accommodate a turning ox-wagon and its 16 oxen. Deep storm drains, whose function was to carry away surplus water in the rainy season, made cars lurch alarmingly as they drove over them. On the outskirts tarmacadam gave way to strip roads (two strips of tarmacadam), then finally to the minor roads to dirt, which was thrown up in clouds as cars sped along. Official buildings had red-tiled roofs, whitewashed walls, long verandas (*stoeps*) and Union Jacks flying from flagpoles in their forecourts. Bungalows—invariably occupied by whites—had whitewashed walls, with a dark red band around the bottom to disguise the mud that splashed up when the rains came.

The seasons were classified as cool (April to August), hot (September to mid–November), and rainy (mid–November to March).In the hot season, green lawns were kept maintained by water sprinklers and looked incongruous, surrounded as they were by such arid, dusty land.

Settlements, small and large, were surrounded by waist-high grass (the "Bush," or "veld"—the Afrikaans word for open, unforested grassland), bare in places and dotted with trees, such as mimosa, mopani, wild fig and kaffir orange. In September, the leaves of the massassa trees burst forth, and the whole veld became a sea of red and gold.

Black house servants lived in *kais*, tiny two-room dwellings situated at the bottom of the garden. One room was for ablutions and the other was the bedroom with palliasses on the floor. Water was available from an outside standpipe. All black males were called "Boy," no matter their age. As servants in the white households, they appeared resplendent in spotless white uniforms (instead of the usual drab khaki), with coffee and cream cakes borne on silver trays with damask cloths. The blacks addressed the whites as "baas" or "madam," and called their children "piccanin baas" or "piccanin madam." The servants were given meat three times a week and maize every day.

As far as leisure time was concerned, blacks were given one day off per week and one weekend off per month. They were immensely hospitable to one another, calling each other "brother" or "sister," accommodating visitors in their cramped kais or else visiting their families on the native reserves.

As for the whites, the town of Gwelo was supplied with water and hydroelectric power by nearby Whitewaters Dam. Lizards three feet or more in length with brilliant turquoise or yellow undersides could be seen at the dam, darting across the sunbaked rocks from one granite boulder to another.

Beside the dam was a swimming pool—to swim in the dam itself would have been folly because of a disease called bilharzia, which was found in all Rhodesian lakes and rivers except for those in the mountainous region of Inyanga in the eastern districts. There, the waters were too cold for the parasitic worm that causes the disease to survive. Bilharzia can damage the liver and spleen and can cause anemia, even cancer of the bladder. Those brave enough to venture in their motorboats up the river, which was the source of the dam, were likely to find a crocodile or a snake swimming along beside them!

The dream of every black person was to own a bicycle, and to this end employees would pool their wages so that every month the person at the top of the list could go into town to purchase a gleaming new machine. The more employees there were, the longer the wait, which might be up to two or three years!

For those blacks who chose not to obey the law, however, the penalty could be quite harsh. A common sight in the 1950s was the arrival of the "banditi," a dozen or so convicts, each barefoot and attired in red-and-white shirts of varying length—some almost reaching to the knee—and khaki shorts that had clearly seen better days. In charge of the banditi were two soldiers, a sergeant and a corporal dressed immaculately in the uniform of the Rhodesian African Rifles and armed with shotguns. All of those in the group were black: in Southern Rhodesia there was segregation even in the prison system. The banditi would present themselves at some public building and the sergeant, standing proudly erect and beaming, would inquire of the official in charge, "What jobs have you for my boys today, baas?" "Clearing the scrub-land" was the usual reply. During the conversation, it was not unusual for the sergeant to give his shotgun to one of the banditi. Then, as his men worked away with their mattocks, singing in unison as they did so and removing every single stone and weed in their path, the sergeant would enjoy one of Rhodesia's most important products—cigarettes—which were one halfpenny each at that time.

The first European to grow tobacco in Rhodesia was Dunbar Moodie in the 1890s, and it was first cultivated commercially in 1902 by a Dr. Sketchley, who had previously grown the crop in Fiji. The leaves were dried in enormous sheds where, having been hung up for the prescribed period, they turned from green to yellow. Then a large number of native women were employed in sorting it according to its quality.

Primary education for blacks was provided at mission schools and at government schools situated in the townships and in the native reserves. By the 1950s 90 percent of blacks in Southern Rhodesia had learned to read and write in their own language. Secondary education was another matter, there being far more high schools for whites than there were for blacks. However, the Goromonzi High School near Salisbury, which opened in 1946, prepared native students for the Cambridge School Certificate (equivalent to "Ordinary level") and for the Higher School Certificate ("Advanced level"). In 1958 another secondary school for blacks, the Fletcher High School, opened near the town of Gwelo.

The landscape of Southern Rhodesia at the time was spectacular. The Sabi River rose in Northern Rhodesia to flow down through Mashonaland and the foothills of the Chimanimani Mountains into Mozambique, to the waters of the Indian Ocean, which it joined near the port of Bartolomeu Dias. At the point where it was spanned by the silver Birchenough Bridge (named after Sir Henry Birchenough, one-time president of the BSAC), the river was 1,000 feet wide. Because the Sabi valley was situated on the low veld, temperatures here could reach as high as 117 degrees in the shade. Little did blacks or whites suspect that, within two decades, this region would resound to the bomb blasts and gunfire of a bloody civil war.

During the 1950s, white immigration into Southern Rhodesia, a prosperous country with a stable government and an excellent climate and fine scenery, doubled to over 200,000 people per year. Nevertheless, tensions were beginning to mount. In 1958, Garfield Todd was deposed as its prime minister for exhibiting pro-black traits, and elections brought Sir Edgar Whitehead of the United Federal Party to power. In Northern Rhodesia in the same year, Kenneth Kaunda founded the Zambian African National Congress.

Although newcomers to Rhodesia quickly adapted to the new way of life, those with foresight were aware of the basic unfairness of the situation pertaining in the country and knew in their hearts that it could not last forever. For example, in the 1950s white people would not have considered entertaining blacks in their homes, taking blacks for rides in their cars, or spending leisure time with them. Gwelo, like any medium-sized English town, had all the amenities—library, swimming pool, department stores, hospital, post office, municipal buildings and so forth. However, unlike an English town these buildings all bore a notice in English—"WHITES ONLY"—and below that, in Afrikaans, "SLEGS VIR BLANKES."

Robert Mugabe, in the Southern Rhodesia of the 1950s, would have been only too familiar with this system of racial segregation, which was all-pervasive there. Apartheid (this word is Afrikaans and means "separateness"), as it was commonly known, had been officially sanctioned in South Africa since 1924 when James Hertzog became prime minister. It became the official policy of the government of that country from 1948 on, when the National Party came to power under Prime Minister Daniel Malan. This policy of aparteid continued with Malan's successors, Johannes Strijdom (1954–58) and Hendrik Verwoerd (1958–66). A similar policy had been in operation in Rhodesia since 1933, when Prime Minister Godfrey Huggins had advocated racial segregation.

Because of what was happening in other African countries and those even further afield, it seemed obvious to anyone coming from a democratic country that before long there would inevitably be "one man, one vote," and there would be black majority rule in Rhodesia. After all, the Gold Coast was about to become the first of Britain's African colonies to achieve independence, and the others would surely follow. However, at any suggestion of this, there were howls of protest from the white Rhodesians, who said they would rather die than hand the country over to the blacks. They had convinced themselves that their position of power was how it was—and always would be! The Afrikaners in particular seemed not to be aware of the strength of the tide of black nationalist aspirations that threatened to engulf them. Britain also seemed behind the times when, in November 1956, acting out the role of the great colonial power it had once been, it invaded the Suez Canal. The truth was that for many, the process by which Britain was divesting itself of its former colonies seemed to be painfully slow, and in the meantime most black Rhodesians had no vote, no property of their own, and no prospect of ever having either.

What about the three British colonies to the north of Rhodesia? The British Protectorate of Uganda would soon achieve internal self-government without strife. A United Nations trusteeship governed by Britain, together with Julius Nyerere and his Tanganyikan African National Union were campaigning then for independence in Tanganyika, and they would succeed. However, in Kenya there had been great unrest since 1952, when the Mau Mau (a Kikuyu secret society) had begun a terrorist campaign to drive white farmers off their land. The following year Jomo Kenyatta, leader of the Kenyan African Union, was imprisoned by the British. Rumors spread that the whole continent of Africa would be subjected to a Communist takeover, and these fears were exploited by die-hard whites who wished to hold on to power.

Further north still, a bitter war was being fought in Algeria between the National Independence Front and the French colonial army. In Cyprus, a terrorist campaign was being waged by the Greek Cypriots against British rule, in favor of "Enosis" (union with Greece).

In Mozambique, an overseas province of Portugal on Southern Rhodesia's eastern border, the struggle for independence was still some way off. In South Africa, still a member of the Commonwealth at the time, the ANC had been formed by former students of schools run by missionaries in order to campaign for the rights of the black majority. In 1950, following the passing of the Group Areas Act, which segregated blacks from whites, the ANC had begun a campaign of civil disobedience. On the white side, there was much talk about a secret organization of Afrikaners called the Broederbond, which had pledged itself to resist a black takeover to the last.

3

Mugabe's Formative Years

Mugabe's upbringing by Jesuit priests imbued him with a spirit of discipline and a knowledge of the ten commandments. An intelligent young man, he would have been well aware of the harsh world that existed outside the confines of the Mission: conditions for blacks in the Salisbury area could be particularly harsh. Natives working on the tobacco farms in the region started work at 4 A.M. and finished at 10 or 11 P.M. Their wages were a pittance, and they were mainly fed beans. There was no adequate supply of drinking water nor any proper housing. Diseases such as kwashiorkor (caused by protein deficiency), marasmus (wasting of the body from starvation), and diarrhea were common. Long queues of blacks were to be found outside the chemist shops; if a white person came in, a black person had to step aside, which meant sometimes waiting a full day for medicine. A black person caught without a pass (*satupa*) faced a beating, and if they were unwise enough to stray into Portuguese Mozambique they risked having their hands cut off, for this was an offense. It was a well-known fact that the son of a white tobacco baron had beaten one of his black employees to death for not cleaning his (the baron's) shoes thoroughly. For this crime the baron's son received a derisorily short prison sentence.

On the other hand, Mugabe would have been inspired to hear from Father O'Hea about Ireland's struggle for independence from

Britain; one which Mugabe probably noticed was achieved not with the pen but with the sword; or, in this case, the gun.

After Mugabe's father walked out and his two older brothers had died, a period of initial numbness for Mugabe, together with an urge to deny the reality of these catastrophic events, would have given way to anxiety, anger and despair. Mugabe may then have turned inwards, blamed himself for what had happened, and felt immensely guilty. He may also have agonized as to whether his father Gabriel would ever return, particularly as he had cut himself off and failed to support his family. A trait of a child who has been cut off from one or both parents is that of detachment: because he or she is unwilling to risk being let down again, he or she becomes self-sufficient and is able to relate to others only on a superficial level.

Mugabe realized that one way he could regain control of his life was by working hard for his teacher-training qualification. This would enable him to earn the money that would provide him a degree of independence. After he achieved this, he then, to his credit, shouldered the responsibility for his mother and siblings, and also for his father who eventually returned home and for his half-siblings.

Fort Hare University would have been an inspiration to Mugabe, for there were nationalists there who were determined to overthrow the apartheid regime in South Africa, and who were already developing the infrastructure and making the contacts to achieve this.

In 1957 Ghana was about to become the first British African colony to achieve independence, and Kwame Nkrumah (soon to be its first president) invited educated Africans to come to his country to study, teach, and derive support for their own nationalistic aspirations. Mugabe duly availed himself of this opportunity of earning more money to support his family, and in June 1958 he took up a post as teacher on a four-year contract at St. Mary's Teacher Training College in Takoradi. In Ghana he saw Africans "being made directors of companies, headmasters of schools, heads of departments," and so forth. It was here in Ghana that he "accepted the general principles of Marxism."[1] Also, at the age of 34, he met his wife-to-be, Sally Heyfron, a 25-year-old Ghanaian teacher whose family had made it their business to look after the Africans whom Nkrumah had invited there.

In September 1957 the City Youth League, dedicated to confrontation with whites rather than cooperation, and the ANC of Bulawayo, which was founded in the 1930s but had since lapsed into obscurity, combined to form the ANC of Rhodesia. Its chosen leader was 40-year-old Joshua Nkomo, a farmer's son and preacher from Matabeleland. Contrary to popular belief, Nkomo was not of Ndebele origin: he was a member of the Karanga people who were related to the Shona. Having received his education in South Africa, Nkomo returned to Rhodesia in 1945, worked for the railways, and became leader of the Union of Black Rhodesia Railway Workers in 1951. In that year, he also obtained an external B.A. degree from the University of South Africa in Johannesburg.

People flocked to join the ANC, which began to challenge the decisions of white native commissioners. Matters came to a head when a court action was initiated against the prime minister himself, Sir Edgar Whitehead of the United Federal Party, who was accused of misusing the 1951 Land Husbandry Act against blacks. Throughout the land, storm clouds were gathering. Opposition by Africans to the Federation erupted early in 1959, when the ANC began a campaign of violence and intimidation in its three component territories.

On February 26, 1959, the government declared a state of emergency in Southern Rhodesia: the African nationalist parties were banned, and 300 of its members including its leaders were imprisoned. However, Joshua Nkomo, who was visiting Egypt at the time, was not captured. Nkomo moved on to London and did not return to Rhodesia until November 1960, when he was restricted to the Semokwe reserve south of Bulawayo.

As a result of the unrest, Sir Patrick Devlin, a senior High Court judge, was sent from England as head of an independent commission, which reported to the government of Harold Macmillan in July that the root cause of the discontent was the dislike of the natives for the Federation.

In Nyasaland, the situation was even worse. The leader of the African nationalists there was Dr. Hastings Banda, who had returned to his country in 1958 after 42 years spent in the United States and Britain. An outbreak of rioting in Nyasaland in late February 1959 obliged its governor, Sir Robert Armitage, to request assistance from

British and Federal territorial troops and police. The result was that 51 black people were killed by the security forces, and Banda and 1,200 of his supporters were arrested and their Malawi Congress Party banned. Banda would be imprisoned in Gwelo, where he would remain until his release the following April. The hatred now displayed by many whites toward Dr. Banda was only equaled by the indignation felt by the blacks about the treatment of their countrymen by their rulers. These events set alarm bells ringing in the minds of many white Rhodesians, who became anxious not only for their own future but for that of their children.

By late 1959, most of the ANC detainees had been released, but as the organization was still proscribed, the National Democratic Party (NDP) was launched on New Year's Day, 1960. Its avowed aim was not simply to achieve political representation but to abolish the Constitution itself, which was the source of all discriminatory legislation. One of its leaders was Ndabaningi Sithole whose book *African Nationalism* stated the case for the nationalist cause. Leopold Takawira, a founding member of the NDP, said, "We are no longer asking Europeans to rule us well, we now want to rule ourselves."[2] (Takawira was a Catholic teacher whom Mugabe had known from his student days at Katuma Mission.)

British Prime Minister Harold Macmillan demonstrated his understanding of the aspirations of black nationalists throughout the continent when, in a speech he made in Cape Town in February 1960, he spoke of the "wind of change" that was blowing through Africa. "The growth of national [black] consciousness is a political fact," he said. Macmillan would have been well aware in any case that attempts to halt the tide were futile, as the French were discovering in their fight against FLN nationalists in Algeria. Only a month later, on March 21, blacks at Sharpeville, 40 miles south of Johannesburg, demonstrated peacefully against the pass laws, which were designed to restrict their movement and exclude them from urban areas without good reason. Sixty-nine protestors were shot dead by the police— many in the back as they were fleeing.

Dr. Banda was released from prison in Southern Rhodesia in April 1960. Ian Macleod, leader of the British House of Commons, had argued that "paradoxically," Banda was "the most likely African

Nyasa to keep Nyasaland within the Federation."[3] Banda duly returned home, no further violence occurred, and the state of emergency in his country was lifted. The following month, Mugabe returned home to Salisbury on leave and soon found himself involved in the political struggle.

In July 1960, Leopold Takawira and three other NDP officials were arrested and charged under the Unlawful Organisations Act. The next day, a crowd marched 8 miles from the black suburb of Highfield into Salisbury, in the hopes that Prime Minister Whitehead would meet their delegation. However, the marchers were stopped by riot police at Stoddart Hall in the black township of Harare. This became known as the "March of the 7,000." The Morning after that, half the black labor force of the Salisbury district failed to turn up for work; instead they joined their comrades at Stoddart Hall, swelling the number of marchers to 40,000. Whitehead, however, refused to meet the delegation and called up a local battalion of the territorial militia. That afternoon, Mugabe addressed the crowd, who applauded heartily when he told them about Ghana and about his vision that one day Rhodesia would emulate that country. He was beginning to make his way in the world, and he would one day feature in events more dramatic than anyone could imagine.

The next day the police moved in. They arrested 130 blacks and wounded many others, some seriously. The following weekend, the unrest spread to Bulawayo, where 11 blacks were shot. The government reacted by passing the Law and Order (Maintenance) Amendment Act, which gave the police virtually unlimited powers to deal with the demonstrators. In the words of the Federation's highly respected chief justice, Sir Robert Tredgold, who resigned in protest because of this Act, which effectively abolished human rights for blacks: "This bill outrages every basic right. If passed into law, it will remove the last vestige of doubt about whether Rhodesia is a police state."[4]

Ian Douglas Smith and Mugabe were the chief protagonists in the struggle that ensued. Smith, the son of a butcher, was born in Selukwe and was educated at Chaplin School in Gwelo and Rhodes University in South Africa, where he graduated with a B.A. degree in commerce. In World War II, Smith served as a pilot in 237 (Rhodesia)

Ian Smith (photograph courtesy of *The Observer*).

Squadron and in 130 Squadron, RAF, and he returned to Rhodesia in 1946. In 1948, as a member of the Rhodesia Party, Smith was elected as member for Selukwe (where he was a farmer) in the Southern Rhodesia Legislative Assembly. In 1953, he entered the Federal Parliament as the United Federal Party's member for Midlands, and in 1956 was appointed chief whip under Prime Minister Roy Welensky.

Mugabe was under pressure to resign from his teaching post in Ghana and return to Rhodesia, which he did in May 1960. His role then was to galvanize the NDP and in particular its Youth Wing, which would encourage the younger generation to commit themselves to the aims of the Party.

Mugabe's sojourn in Ghana would have given him hope and encouragement. Here was a country about to become independent from Britain: where blacks for the first time would have a fair chance in life to pursue whatever job or career they chose. In October 1960 he was elected as the NDP's secretary for information and publicity. He was also editor of *The Democratic Voice*, the NDP's mouthpiece.

Southern Rhodesia's 1961 Constitution (worked out between Whitehead's ruling United Federal Party and the British government), did not please Smith, who resigned from the federal government in protest. The reason, as Smith stated, was the "all-important omission" that there was no "guarantee of our independence in the event of a break-up of the Federation."[5] In fact, when the Constitution was drafted, the British inserted Section III, which reserved them the right to intervene by Order-in-Council: a right which would only be removed at final independence.

Under this Constitution, whites would have 50 seats (the "A Roll") and blacks would have 15 seats (the "B Roll") in the Rhodesian Parliament. However, if a black acquired sufficient property, income, and educational qualifications, he or she would be eligible to submit himself or herself for election to the A Roll. In theory, this opened up the possibility of eventual black majority rule.[6]

In April 1961, Mugabe and Sarah "Sally" Francesca Heyfron, a convert to Catholicism, were married at the Roman Catholic Church in Harare. That year, the Foreign Office convened a constitutional conference in Salisbury under Commonwealth Secretary Duncan Sandys. There, Nkomo, Sithole, and Herbert Chitepo (chairman of

ZANU and commander of its forces), agreed on the so-called 1961 Constitution. The whites would give the blacks 15 seats in a 65-seat Parliament, and there would be no more interference by Britain in Rhodesia's constitutional affairs. However, in order to be established on the B Roll, a black person would be required to have an income of £240 per annum for the previous 6 months or ownership of immovable property to the value of £450 (or a lesser amount if he or she was over the age of 30) and two years' secondary education. This would be beyond the wildest dreams of all but a few.

This deal was swiftly rejected by Nkomo's NDP executive. Mugabe described it as a sellout. "Europeans must realise that unless the legitimate demands of African nationalism are recognised," said Mugabe, "then racial conflict is inevitable." The government's reaction was predictable. In December 1961 the NDP was banned, its funds seized, and its leaders prohibited from addressing any public meetings for four months. Within ten days of the ban Nkomo responded by replacing the NDP with the Zimbabwe African Peoples Union (ZAPU), in which Mugabe once again fulfilled the role of publicity secretary, and also the position of secretary-general. This was the year that South Africa declared itself a republic and left the Commonwealth.

In 1962 Ian Smith founded the right-wing Rhodesian Front Party, and Marandellas tobacco farmer Winston Field (formerly the leader of the Dominion Party) became its first leader. A backer of the Rhodesian Front was multimillionaire tobacco baron Douglas Collard "Boss" Lilford. Like other farming magnates, many of whom were members of Parliament, he saw it as a means of maintaining a cheap labor force of blacks; he also opposed Edgar Whitehead's plans for greater political representation for blacks, and for their integration into schools, hospitals and residential areas.

In September 1962, the government responded to the creation of ZAPU by banning it and placing its leaders under a three-month restriction order: Mugabe was sent to a tribal reserve 50 miles from Salisbury. For the nationalists, this meant a loss of funds, property, and vehicles, which they could ill afford.

On December 14, 1962, just as the ZAPU leaders, including Mugabe, were being freed, Edgar Whitehead's progressive policies proved too much for the white electorate to bear. In the election the Rhodesian Front took over as the government party with Winston Field as prime minister and Ian Smith as his deputy prime minister and minister of finance. In the same month, another constitutional conference was convened to prepare Nyasaland for independence with black majority rule.

In March 1964, Mugabe traveled to Northern Rhodesia to address a meeting of that country's United National Independence Party. He described recent amendments to the Law and Order (Maintenance) Act (the so-called hanging bill, which said that any person found guilty of throwing an explosive object at a building, whether such a building was occupied at the time or not, would be mandatorily sentenced to death), as "the legalisation of murder." Consequently, three months later when he returned home, he was arrested, charged with "making a subversive statement within the hearing of others," and released on bail. His wife, Sally, who had criticized Britain for abandoning the blacks, was also arrested and charged with making subversive statements. She had made a speech in which she attacked Britain for abandoning Rhodesia's blacks and said, "The Queen can go to hell."[7]

When restrictions on Nkomo were lifted in January 1963, Mugabe traveled abroad to drum up support for his Party before returning home at the end of March, when he persuaded his ZAPU executive to leave Rhodesia and relocate its headquarters to the Tanganyikan capital, Dar-es-Salaam. Mugabe, who was anxious to demonstrate to the people that he and his colleagues were as willing to make sacrifices as they were, was opposed to the idea in principle, but he nevertheless concurred. While awaiting his trial for subversion, Mugabe fled Rhodesia to join his colleagues at Dar-es-Salaam.[8] As for Sally, she had served a nine-month jail sentence and was also out on bail, pending an appeal. Another concern was that Sally was pregnant again, having lost her first child at birth.

On their arrival in Tanganyika, the ZAPU leaders, contrary to what Nkomo had led them to believe, discovered that its president, Julius Nyerere, considered Nkomo's decision to leave Rhodesia to be ill-advised. They therefore returned to Rhodesia, except for Mugabe, who remained in Dar-es-Salaam for the birth of his son,

The Reverend Ndabaningi Sithole (photograph courtesy of Rod Cox).

Nhamodzenyika (in Shona, the "suffering country"). On July 4, 1963, a constitutional conference was held at Victoria Falls to prepare Northern Rhodesia for independence.

The Tanganyikan episode convinced some members of ZAPU, Mugabe included, that Nkomo was inept and lacked leadership ability. Nkomo for his part suspended four "rebel" members of his executive committee, including Party Chairman Washington Malianga, Sithole, Takawira, and Mugabe. On August 8, 1963, as a result of this schism, the Zimbabwe African National Union (ZANU) was created, with the Reverend Ndabaningi Sithole as president. Mugabe, a founding member, was elected in his absence as the party's secretary-general.

Nkomo's ZAPU drew support mainly from the Ndebele people of urban Salisbury, and from Bulawayo, the capital of Matabeleland: the Ndebele people were 20 percent of the country's population. Sithole's ZANU, however, drew its support mainly from the Shona peoples of the south, the east and the Midlands. Unlike ZAPU, ZANU dedicated itself from the beginning to armed conflict.

Having enjoyed the company of his infant child for only three months, Mugabe returned home in December 1963, was arrested and then remanded in custody until his trial. Meanwhile, rather than have his wife face a prison sentence back in Rhodesia, Mugabe persuaded Sally to return to Ghana with the baby to her parents' home.

The terms of the detention order were as follows: "Whereas under the terms of Section 50 of the Law and Order (Maintenance) Act, certain powers are vested in me, and whereas certain information has been placed before me and whereas due to confidential information which I cannot reveal, I am satisfied that you are likely to commit acts of violence throughout Rhodesia...." This was signed by Justice Minister Desmond Lardner-Burke. In August 1964, Mugabe was sent to Salisbury's maximum security prison "until this order is revoked or otherwise varied by me [Lardner-Burke]." He would spend the next 11 years in various prisons.

Following Mugabe's arrest and imprisonment, about 150 ZAPU and ZANU leaders were also detained, including Nkomo himself, who was sent to a detention center at Gonakudzingwa in the southeast of the country. Nkomo would remain in prison for ten years.

ZANU and ZAPU, each anxious to bolster support and by intimidation if necessary, became increasingly hostile to one another. Mobs rampaged through the black townships of Salisbury and through some of the tribal trust lands; there were assaults, bombings, arson and stonings.

Mugabe, who was acknowledged to be a solitary person, was nevertheless eloquent, literate and intellectually rigorous in debate. As a fervent believer in the cause of equality for blacks, and with clear ideas as to what was fair and acceptable when negotiating the future of his country with Rhodesian and British politicians, he was a natural choice to rally the ZANU faithful and was destined to achieve high office quickly. Sally was also genuinely interested in and concerned for the welfare of the ordinary people of Zimbabwe. She worked hard on their behalf.

4

Imprisonment

At Salisbury, six men shared a dark and squalid cell with too few beds and a bucket for slopping out. Here they were incarcerated for 23 hours a day: sickness and death were their constant companions. Study was forbidden to Mugabe, and he was initially denied access to written material. At Wha Wha near Gwelo, conditions were equally harsh. Sikombela at Que Que was a barbed wire enclosure where the guards lived in houses built by the government, but the prisoners were left to build their own houses. Mugabe was honored by having his hut (a *daga*, made of mud and straw with a thatched roof) built for him by the other prisoners. Food consisted of meat, beans, and maize-meal, which was cooked to make the traditional "sadza" porridge.

Outside the prison walls, white opinion was hardening. In April 1964, Winston Field, who in his Party's eyes had not applied sufficient pressure on the British government to recognize Southern Rhodesia's right to full independence, resigned as prime minister and was succeeded by Ian Smith. Field, like his predecessor Godfrey Huggins, was an Englishman and considered too gentlemanly and deferential to the British: he was someone who, in common parlance, was liable to sell the white Rhodesians down the river. Smith on the other hand, was born and bred in Rhodesia; he was a man of action, whose face still bore the scars from burns received in the course of duty with the Royal Air Force during World War II. The wisdom of Smith's judgment remained to be seen, for it was his constant vow that there would never be black majority rule in his lifetime.

In June 1964, Sithole joined Mugabe in prison. In August, faced with continuing internecine strife between ZANU and ZAPU, Ian Smith, the new leader of the Rhodesia Front Party, banned both parties and arrested their leaders. During his incarceration, Mugabe was determined to keep his mind occupied, and those of his comrades also. With himself as nominal headmaster, and using books donated by charities such as Christian Aid and Christian Care, he created a school wherein prisoners with some education taught those with little or none. Meanwhile Northern Rhodesia became independent as Zambia under President Kenneth Kaunda; Nyasaland as Malawi, under President Hastings Banda.

In the autumn of 1964, Harold Wilson's Labour Party came to power in Britain and tried desperately to prevent the impending white breakaway. In Rhodesia, Smith gathered together a council (*indaba*) of black chiefs—almost all of whom were government employees— and announced afterwards that all 622 of the chiefs were in favor of independence under his 1961 Constitution; Smith ignored the fact that the only true referendum involved enfranchisement of the whole population, on the basis of "one man, one vote."

In October, in a final attempt to find common ground, Wilson himself flew to Salisbury to talk to Smith, and also to talk to Nkomo and Sithole who were released from prison for the occasion. However, the two nationalist leaders, although they initially said they would accept it, quickly changed their minds and rejected Smith's 1961 Constitution, which they had played no part in formulating. Denis Healey, Harold Wilson's defense secretary, realized that armed intervention by Britain had to be ruled out on the grounds that the nearest operational base to that country was Aden; also, British troops might have grave reservations about fighting their own "kith and kin."[1]

In May 1965, Ian Smith felt sufficiently confident to call a general election. It was a total victory for his Rhodesia Front Party, which won all 50 white seats in Parliament. One person who did not support Smith, however, was former prime minister Garfield Todd who, with his family, was under house arrest on his farm at Hokuni. Under the Tribal Trust Lands Act of that year, the native reserves became known as tribal trust lands with trustees created to manage them. The Rhodesian Constitution of 1965 provided no further representation for blacks in Parliament. The number of A Roll seats remained at 50, and the number of B Roll seats remained at 15.

In his negotiations with Wilson, Smith fought for the same objective as had led him to resign from the federal government in 1961: a guarantee of Southern Rhodesia's full and unconditional independence from Britain. When Wilson responded by offering a Royal Commission on the subject, and at the same time made it clear that he would not be

Sir Harold Wilson (photograph courtesy of *The Observer*).

bound by the findings of this Commission, Smith became exasperated. However, the British position was that the terms for independence must be "acceptable to the people of Rhodesia as a whole," and so Wilson can hardly be blamed for refusing to accept what the moderate black nationalist representatives of the overwhelming majority now rejected. On October 29, 1965, Wilson announced publicly that he would not use military force even if Smith unilaterally broke away from Britain. Smith took this as a green light.[2]

When security was suddenly strengthened at Sikombela and Mugabe asked the reason why, he was told by the warders what he had always feared and predicted—Ian Smith, on November 11, 1965, had made a Unilateral Declaration of Independence (UDI). Not everyone shared Smith's vision of a utopian Rhodesia after the UDI. Some were horrified and believed it would be a disaster. Smith subsequently claimed that the decision by himself and the Cabinet to vote for a UDI had been unanimous. This was not the case. Cabinet Minister Harry Reedman, for one, always denied that he had voted in favor of it.

In that year, Garfield Todd applied to leave the country for Scotland, so that he could lead a teach-in at Edinburgh University in order to educate the British public about what he perceived as the iniquities of white rule in Rhodesia. His application was refused. He was arrested, detained in police custody, and then placed under house arrest.

Britain imposed sanctions, culminating in an oil embargo, which the Rhodesians managed to circumvent by importing oil through Mozambique rather than South Africa, as they had done hitherto.

Sympathetic warders smuggled letters out to ZANU Chairman Herbert Chitepo, who was in Lusaka, Zambia, establishing guerrilla bases and preparing for battle. In 1966, 14 ZANU guerrillas infiltrated Rhodesia from Zambia and raided a farm near Hartley, 50 miles from Salisbury, murdering the farmer and his wife. All the insurgents were subsequently killed by the Rhodesian security forces. This incident led the government to transfer the ZANU executive and 30 other ZANU detainees to the remand section of Salisbury's Central Prison; there Mugabe remained for another 8 years. Meanwhile, Smith and Wilson held further unsuccessful talks aboard the HMS *Tiger* in Gibraltar. In that year Britain invoked a United Nations mandate to use its Royal Navy to blockade the Mozambique port of Beira, the terminus for Rhodesia's vital oil pipeline.

George Thomson, Wilson's minister without portfolio, flew to Salisbury for talks on November 7, 1966, with Mugabe, Takawira, and Sithole. When asked by Mugabe why the British had failed to act against an illegal seizure of power by the white regime, Thomson's reply was that Britain had ruled out the use of force.

At Salisbury, Mugabe continued to study for his examinations— despite the harsh conditions. "I do it for myself and Zimbabwe," he said, "because I know that one day we both will need these degrees."[3] He acquired three more degrees by correspondence course from the University of London, including a law degree and a B.A. in administration, bringing his number of degrees to seven.

Late in 1966, an inspector of the Rhodesian police arrived at the prison with Mugabe's sister to tell him that his son, Nhamodzenyika, then 3, had died of cerebral malaria at the home of his wife's parents in Ghana. Mugabe was inconsolable. He begged the prison governor to grant him parole to attend the funeral in Accra, the Ghanaian capital, but Ian Smith intervened personally to prevent this.

The year 1967–68 saw further incursions of guerrilla groups into Rhodesia from Zambia, but they met with little success. In October 1968, Smith and Wilson held talks aboard HMS *Fearless,* again in Gibraltar, and again these talks proved fruitless. Funded by the Ariel Education Initiative—devoted to excellence in teaching and learning in inner-city schools—Sally moved to London to study for a degree in home economics at London University's Queen Elizabeth College.

In 1969 Smith introduced a new Republican Constitution, which was drawn up unilaterally without the participation of the British government. Unlike the previous Constitutions of 1961 and 1965, this removed the previous criteria, so that the basis by which blacks could achieve representation in Parliament was determined solely by the amount of tax that they contributed to the Exchequer. As that figure was then less than 1 percent, the prospect of black majority rule became virtually nonexistent. In Smith's own words, the 1969 Constitution "sounded the death knell of the notion of majority rule,"[4] and "would entrench government in the hands of civilised Rhodesians for all time."[5] Smith also introduced the Land Tenure Act. That Act stated that henceforward, "for all time," the white and black areas would each contain 45 million acres; the remaining 6 million acres would be designated as national parks and game reserves.

The Reverend Sithole had damned himself in Mugabe's eyes when, in 1969, he renounced the armed struggle against white Rhodesia. In Salisbury Prison, prison authorities caught Sithole in the act of throwing oranges over the wall to Party members posing as visitors. Concealed in these oranges were written instructions for the assassination of Prime Minister Smith. Sithole was brought to trial in January 1969 and charged with conspiracy to murder Smith. He was found guilty and sentenced to six years' imprisonment. Sithole's supporters had already become disaffected and, when the presidency of the party was put to the vote, Sithole was deposed and Robert Mugabe was declared leader of ZANU.

In June 1970 the conservative government came to power in Britain, led by Sir Alec Douglas-Home, and it reached agreement with the Smith regime on the basis of the Republican Constitution introduced by Ian Smith in 1969. When Douglas-Home visited Salisbury and the African leaders were released from prison for him to hear their views, Mugabe told him in no uncertain terms that the Africans rejected the 1969 Constitution and were going to fight for their rights. Then, after a commission sent to Zimbabwe and chaired by Lord Pearce reported that "the people of Rhodesia as a whole do not regard the proposals [Smith's] as a basis for independence," the partnership fell apart.[6] In the same year, Takawira died in prison of undiagnosed diabetes.

Over the next two years, Mugabe heard off and on that the FRELIMO (Front for the Liberation of Mozambique) nationalist guerrillas were making slow but sure progress in their war against the Portuguese colonial government; by 1972 they controlled large areas of the north of the country. By this time ZANU had created a military wing, the Zimbabwe African National Liberation Army (ZANLA). Composed mainly of Shona people, it made common cause with FRELIMO and, backed by Communist China, Yugoslavia, and Romania, began to operate from FRELIMO-controlled territory in Mozambique. On December 21, 1972, ZANLA guerrillas attacked a Rhodesian farmhouse in the Centenary District near Salisbury, blowing up a truck with a land mine when it came to investigate and thereby killing a white corporal. South Africa responded by dispatching a large number of combat police to bolster Rhodesia's defenses.

Nkomo, on the other hand, had established in Zambia ZAPU's military wing, which was backed by the Soviet Union and East Germany and consisted mainly of Ndebele people. This unit was known as the Zimbabwe People's Revolutionary Army (ZIPRA).

When the Rhodesian prison authorities placed restrictions on study materials for the detainees in the early 1970s, Mugabe, not to be thwarted, sent the references for documents he required to Sally in London; she meticulously tracked them down, transcribed them by hand, line by line, and posted them back to him.

In 1972, Garfield Todd (seen as a dangerous liberal and a threat to the Smith regime) and his daughter, Judith, were imprisoned. He was then confined once more to the family ranch near Bulawayo; Judith would spend the next seven years in exile.

The entire situation in central Africa was changed by General Spinoza's military coup of 1974 in Portugal's capital, Lisbon. He planned to withdraw Portuguese troops from Mozambique and Angola and grant independence to these nations as soon as possible. Up until then, these two Portuguese colonies had provided a white-dominated buffer zone for South Africa. The president of South Africa, John Vorster, realized that soon he would have two newly independent and potentially hostile black African states on his doorstep, with the possibility for guerrilla incursions into his own country. Vorster began a dialogue with Zambia's Kenneth Kaunda, aimed at persuading Smith to end hostilities with ZANU and ZAPU. All political detainees in Rhodesia would be released, and the legality of its nationalist parties would be restored.

In 1974 Mugabe came under pressure to suspend Sithole from the party, and on November 1, ZANU's executive voted for this measure. Mugabe and former ZAPU chairman Malianga were released to attend talks in Lusaka that were designed to prepare the way for a Rhodesian settlement. In attendance were leaders of the so-called Front Line States, such as Tanzania's (formerly Tanganyika, independent since 1961) Julius Nyerere, Zambia's Kenneth Kaunda, leader of Mozambique's nationalists Samora Machel, and Botswana's Seretse Karma, all of whom had supported Nkomo's and Mugabe's war efforts and had allowed guerrilla bases to be established on their territories. As the talks progressed, Mugabe shuttled back and forth to Lusaka by airplane. (On one occasion he was reunited with Sally for the first time in ten years—his wife was so overcome by this that she fainted.) Mugabe was clearly angry with Kaunda, who had arranged a detente with Vorster, and Kaunda in turn was angry about the bickering between the two nationalist parties. Both Kaunda and Nyerere found it difficult to accept that Mugabe, and not Sithole, was the leader of ZANU.

In November 1974, Smith, under more pressure from South Africa, ordered the release of Mugabe, Nkomo and Sithole. Of all the nationalist leaders in all the Commonwealth countries, Mugabe had the unenviable distinction of having spent a longer time in prison—11 years—than anyone else (with the exception of Nelson Mandela). Nkomo took the opportunity to travel widely in Africa and Europe and to promote ZAPU's goal of black majority rule.

Mugabe had been imprisoned without trial, and in prison he would have experienced humiliation and degradation. For over a decade, he had been denied some of his favorite pleasures: watching sport, especially cricket, and listening to traditional Shona music and such singers as Bing Crosby, Elvis Presley and Pat Boone, as well as classical music. He was also denied the freedom to enjoy the beauty of the outside world, Southern Rhodesia in particular, which was a beautiful country.

Mugabe and his wife had already lost one child, and when his second child, 3-year-old Nhamodzenyika, also died, he was inconsolable. Yet the incarceration did not break his spirit; in prison he was determined that not only he himself, but his fellow prisoners also, would furnish their minds with knowledge that would be useful to them should the day ever come when the blacks of Zimbabwe achieved the right to determine their own destiny. He chose his subjects carefully, those which would be useful to him when he resumed his political duties with ZANU, namely law and economics.

He was determined to continue being a teacher, just as he would have done had he been a free man. Knowledge was power, and the prospect of power, however remote, was of vital importance to one who had been stripped of all dignity and denied all other possibility of advancement.

By declaring a UDI in November 1965, Ian Smith flew in the face of all that was going on around him; he tried to turn the clock back in a world where the tide was turning against authoritarian states and dictatorships in favor of democracy. Muzorewa, Sithole and Nkomo were moderate men with whom he could have reached accord, and as for the British government, it had never wavered; the principle of "one man, one vote," had to be implemented before independence was granted. Now, by his action, Smith would drive Mugabe, and also Nkomo, to extremism, and Smith would plunge the country into a bloody civil war.

5

Freedom and Exile

Finally, in December 1974, after ten years and four months, Mugabe was released from prison. In November 1974 there was a rebellion in a ZANU camp at Chifombo on the Zambian-Mozambique border, due to ineffectual military leadership and rivalry between ZANU Chairman Herbert Chitepo (of the Manyika people) and Josiah Tongogara, the Commander in the Field (of the Karangas). Tongogara was dispatched to crush the rebellion, which he did with the loss of 45 lives. However, on March 18, 1975, Chitepo was assassinated in Lusaka by a car bomb. Tongogara was charged, found guilty of the murder, but sentenced to only 18 months' imprisonment.

In March 1975, Sithole was brought before a special tribunal and charged with leading an unlawful organization (ZANU), but in the middle of his trial President Vorster of South Africa intervened, telling Smith that to proceed would damage the chances of peace. Sithole was released, and the following month he attended the Organisation of African Unity (OAU) Foreign Ministers' Conference in Dar-es-Salaam, where he met with Nkomo and Bishop Abel Muzorewa, president of the ANC. Educated in the United States, the 50-year-old Muzorewa was bishop of the United Methodist Church. His ANC favored an internal settlement of the political situation, as opposed to an armed confrontation.

The 49-year-old Mugabe realized that in Rhodesia, as an activist, he was liable to be re-arrested at any moment. Therefore, he and ZANU official and friend Edgar Tekere left secretly in March 1975 for Mozambique, where at Nyafuru, short of the border, they found unexpected allies. Chief Tangwena, who with his 3,000 tribespeople had inhabited the region for centuries, had been displaced by the Rhodesian government, which bulldozed his *kraals* and redesignated his lands to the white community. It was Chief Tangwena's tribesmen who smuggled Mugabe and Tekere across the border one night in late April, into an area where ZANLA guerrillas were based.

Two months later, the war in Mozambique ended, and the country gained its independence from Portugal with Samora Machel as its first president. The release of Sithole, however, meant that the authorities in Mozambique were disinclined to accept Mugabe as the leader of ZANU, and the FRELIMO leaders placed him in protective custody.

When restrictions on Mugabe were lifted, he was free to take up residence in the Mozambique port of Quelimane: from there he visited the north of the country and also Tanzania, where military training camps for the war effort were being created. Meanwhile Nkomo, Sithole and Muzorewa continued to pursue with Smith the policy of detente that Mugabe so despised, but they failed to reach agreement with him at the Victoria Falls Conference of August 1975.

In November ZANU and ZAPU put aside their differences and joined to form the Zimbabwe People's Army (ZIPA), with nine representatives from each on the council of its high command. ZIPA, however, collapsed after brutal clashes between the two rival groups.

Sally Mugabe remained in London until 1975 where, after taking her degree, she worked for the Runnymede Trust—devoted to the fight against social injustice and racial discrimination. She lobbied members of Parliament for her husband's release and for support for her country of adoption.

In January 1976 almost 1,000 guerrillas infiltrated Southern Rhodesia's eastern border and attacked white farms. The Rhodesians responded by drafting all men over the age of 38 for compulsory military service. At the end of January, Mugabe traveled to London, where he accused President Kaunda of arresting his men and locking them up "within his prisons and restriction areas."[1]

In February the leaders of the Front Line States visited Mugabe at Quelimane and were told by Nkomo that negotiations with Smith had failed. A few days later, when the Rhodesian Air Force attacked a village just inside Mozambique, Machel closed the border and gave Mugabe permission to use his northern province of Tete as a base for mounting military strikes on Rhodesia.

A month later, in an effort to enlist the help of the outside world, Mugabe went to Switzerland where the Kampfendes Afrika organization presented him with 10,000 Swiss francs. That spring, Machel installed Mugabe and his wife in a Portuguese-style villa near the coast at the capital, Maputo (formerly Lourenco Marques), which would be their home for the next four years. Russian arms traders, by insisting that Mugabe recognize Nkomo as overall leader, drove Mugabe to seek more arms from the Chinese.

Guerrilla infiltrators began intimidating black Rhodesian farmworkers, ordering them to abstain from work and ambushing their company buses if they refused. The Rhodesians responded by disguising themselves as FRELIMO soldiers and attacking the camp at Nyazonia, 35 miles inside Mozambique, where they killed 670 men.

Alarmed by Soviet and Chinese support for the guerrilla armies, U.S. Secretary of State Henry Kissinger got involved, visiting central Africa several times in the summer of 1976. By then, Mugabe was universally recognized as the leader of ZANU by the Front Line States.

At a meeting with the Front Line presidents in September 1976, Mugabe accused Nkomo of pulling his ZAPU troops out of the war and leaving all the fighting to ZANU's military wing, ZANLA. Three weeks later, Smith, under heavy pressure from Kissinger, made a speech to the nation, accepting the principle of majority rule.[2] The following month, ZANU and ZAPU united to form the Patriotic Front, or ZANU-PF, and photographs appeared in the Mozambique newspapers depicting Mugabe with President Machel who, although initially bemused by Mugabe's coup against Sithole, now gave him his full backing.

On October 9, Mugabe and Nkomo issued a joint statement in Dar-es-Salaam, "rejecting the proposals by Dr. Henry Kissinger as a basis for any discussion." They established the Patriotic Front, with the aim of pursuing an "armed liberation struggle until the achievement of victory."[3]

At a conference held in Geneva, Switzerland, on October 28, attended by himself and Nkomo, Mugabe declared that the Rhodesia he envisaged would be "socialist, and [would] draw on the socialist systems of Mozambique and Tanzania."[4] However, he did admit that "one cannot get rid of all the trappings of free enterprise. After all, even the Russians and Chinese have their petit bourgeoisie." He regarded Kissinger's plan as unsatisfactory, in that both the army and the police would remain in the control of the whites. No agreement could be reached as to the timescale for independence, nor with the form that the interim government was to take, so the talks collapsed.

Sally Mugabe, who had studied for a home economics degree with its emphasis on food and nutrition specifically to help the people of Zimbabwe, now busied herself by helping in the guerrilla and refugee camps of northern Mozambique and Tanzania. She also traveled abroad, especially to Scandinavia to raise funds for food, clothing and medicines.

With Tongogara now released from prison and back in command of the war, ZANU guerrillas began to attack soft targets such as St. Paul's Mission at Musami, where 7 missionaries were killed, and a store in Salisbury, where 11 were killed and 76 injured by a bomb explosion. At the same time, volunteers for ZANU poured into Mozambique at the rate of 1,000 per month.

In March 1977, Mugabe complained in Lusaka that not enough material assistance was being given by the "Front Line States, OAU members, and friendly socialist countries" to the Patriotic Front, which he claimed had "a well-planned strategy that would bear immediate results if more aid was forthcoming."[5] On August 31, Mugabe got his final seal of approval when his party's Congress-in-exile proclaimed him president of ZANU.

New Anglo-American initiatives for a settlement, put forward by Britain's Foreign Secretary Dr. David Owen and the United States' U.N. Ambassador Andrew Young were denounced by Mugabe as "imperialist Manoeuvres" that "pay lip-service to the principle of majority rule."[6]

Emnity between Mugabe and Nkomo increased when Mugabe

learned of a secret meeting in late September between Nkomo, Smith, and Kaunda. Mugabe believed that the reason Nkomo had failed to commit all his forces to the war effort was because he was hoping to make a deal with Smith.

At the end of October, Britain's Field Marshal Lord Carver arrived at Dar-es-Salaam, where the idea of a United Nations peace-keeping force to police a cease-fire was mooted. However, in the absence of any detailed plans for a handover of power, both Mugabe and Nkomo rejected the idea. Smith, still anxious to reach agreement with Sithole and Muzorewa ("puppets" of the Smith regime, as Mugabe called them), now struck at Chimoio, deep inside Mozambique, in an attempt to crush Mugabe's guerrilla army. An attempted coup by two leading members of ZANU's central committee was thwarted in the nick of time with the arrest of the ringleaders. Nevertheless, Mugabe refused to condone the execution of these men, despite pressure from other members of the committee.

In November 1977 a war-weary Smith, under pressure from the United States, reached agreement on majority rule with moderate leaders Muzorewa and Sithole: the whites would retain 28 of the 100 parliamentary seats and control of the security forces and treasury.

Talks in Malta in January 1978 between Mugabe, Nkomo, Owen and Young again foundered on the question of who was to control security during the transitional period. In April at Dar-es-Salaam, Cyrus Vance, secretary of state in President Carter's administration, was told by Mugabe that during the transition his forces, which numbered about 40,000 compared to Nkomo's 20,000, must have the dominant role. Meanwhile, white farmers on Zimbabwe's eastern border were being progressively driven from their farms.

Talks between Prime Minister Smith and Bishop Muzorewa for the United African National Council, Senator Chief Chirau for the Zimbabwe United Peoples Organisation and the Reverend Sithole for the African National Council led to the signing of the Internal Constitutional Agreement whereby majority rule was promised by December 31, 1978. By March 1978, the transitional government was established, shortly after which black nationalist ministers were appointed to share the tasks of government with their white counterparts.

Mugabe traveled widely to gain support for his cause; he went to

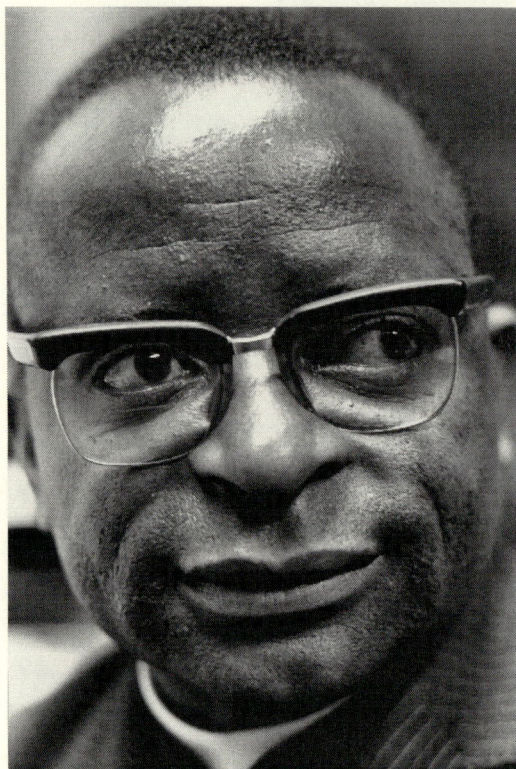

Bishop Abel Muzorewa (photograph courtesy of _The Observer_).

Moscow, Vietnam, North Korea, and Cuba, where Fidel Castro agreed to send military advisors to Mozambique, Angola and Ethiopia to train Mugabe's men. However, a ZANU attack on June 23 on the Elim Mission Station in the Vumba Mountains, in which eight British missionaries were killed and four children (one a baby) were barbarously murdered, drew worldwide condemnation. Mugabe attempted to put the blame for this on Rhodesia's elite special forces unit, the Selous Scouts.

In Lusaka that August, Nkomo again met Smith (without Mugabe's Knowledge). Mugabe was furious with Nkomo and with Zambia's President Kaunda for condoning the meeting, as were Nyerere and Machel. Now it was Nkomo's men who were to gain general opprobrium by shooting down two Viscount Air Rhodesia passenger aircraft with heat-seeking ground-to-air missiles and massacring the survivors; for this the Rhodesian Air Force retaliated by bombing Zambia.

In November 1978 Mugabe visited Italy, where Italian political parties had organized a "Southern Africa Solidarity Conference." He astonished the audience by giving them a lecture on the transformation of Italy from an empire to a democratic state.

In December, ZANU achieved its most spectacular success by blowing up Salisbury's largest fuel depot, causing a five-day fire that destroyed a month's worth of fuel supplies. Hundreds of guerrillas positioned themselves in tribal trust lands near Salisbury, ready to attack.

Mugabe christened 1979 as "The Year of the People's Storm." He was undoubtedly winning the guerrilla war and was adamant that "the final blow, the most decisive knock-out by the people's mailed fist, must be effected soon."[7]

The election, held in April 1979, brought victory to Muzorewa despite the fact that ZANU had nullified his support in the rural areas by forcibly keeping his supporters away from the polling stations. Meanwhile, in Britain, Margaret Thatcher's Conservative Party came to power on May 3 with a large majority.

On June 1, 1979, Muzorewa became both prime minister and minister of defense and combined operations of the government of national unity, with Ian Smith as his minister without portfolio. However, neither black Africa, the United Nations, nor the world at large recognized this new regime.

At the beginning of August 1979, Mugabe sent Edgar Tekere as his representative to the Commonwealth Conference at Lusaka, with a hostile message for the white Rhodesians, for his rival black nationalists, and for Thatcher herself. He referred to "the evil settler racist armed forces," the "treacherous Muzorewa" and Thatcher's "racist mind."[8] Thatcher, however, surprised everyone by declaring her vision of black majority rule, albeit with a permanent white representation in Parliament. The transitional period would be managed "under British Government authority with Commonwealth observers." Finally, in September all parties, including Nkomo, Muzorewa, Ian Smith, and Margaret Thatcher and her Foreign Secretary Lord Carrington converged on London for the Lancaster House Conference. Mugabe attended only reluctantly, after pressure from Kaunda and Machel, who threatened to withdraw their support in the face of damaging raids by the Rhodesians on guerrilla bases in their countries.

Whereas ZANU-PF was heavily committed to the war, Nkomo appeared to be lukewarm, preferring to hold some of his ZAPU troops back rather than send them into action. Mugabe feared that the triumvirate of Nkomo, Sithole and Muzorewa, in conjunction with the white majority, would arrange a package between themselves and the British government that was disadvantageous to the blacks, and which excluded ZANU-PF from the decision-making process. The seemingly endless series of futile negotiations that took place over the years between these parties and himself, and even the Americans when they attempted to break the deadlock, convinced Mugabe that the gun, rather than diplomacy, was the only way to change the status quo.

6

The Lancaster House Conference

At the Lancaster House Conference, held between September and December 1979, there were three delegations: that of the United Kingdom, that of Nkomo and Mugabe, and that of Bishop Muzorewa, which included several whites, including Ian Smith.

It was agreed that Bishop Muzorewa should stand down as prime minister and that Christopher Soames should take charge as British governor, prior to the elections. Lord Soames was a Tory cabinet minister, a former ambassador to France, and the son-in-law of the late Sir Winston Churchill.

On October 18, 1979, Mugabe and Nkomo agreed to the proposed new Constitution, whereby blacks would have 80 seats in the new Parliament and whites, 20. As far as the land issue was concerned, ZANU-PF's understanding of it was as follows: "We have obtained assurances that... Britain, the United States of America and other countries will participate in a multinational donor effort to assist in land, agricultural and economic development programmes. These assurances go a long way in allaying the concern we have over the whole land question, arising from the great need our people have for land and our commitment to satisfy that need when in government."

The great weakness of the Lancaster House Agreement was that

Robert Mugabe (center, with white jacket) with Kenneth Kaunda (second from right, with upraised arm) (photograph courtesy of Rod Cox).

no figure was put down on paper, either actual or notional, as to what sum would be required to compensate the white farmers for their land (although a figure of $2 billion is believed to have been mooted). Also, was it envisaged that all the white farmers would be dispossessed, or would some be allowed to remain in situ? The only relevant passage was that the government could purchase land from a white farmer against that farmer's wishes only if the land was underutilized or required for a public purpose—in that case, the farmer would receive full compensation in foreign exchange.

It was proposed that the governor would keep law and order in the interim by using the existing Rhodesian Police Force, whose commander was General Peter Walls. Mugabe was utterly opposed to this plan. "If ever there was a case for a U.N. peacekeeping force, this was it," he said. "Unless Lord Carrington relents, we will pack our bags and go back to war."[1] Kenneth Kaunda intervened, fearing the effect of any resumption of hostilities on the fragile Zambian economy. The truth was that Zambia, Mozambique and Tanzania had lost the appetite for war. Zambia, in particular, suffered acutely from a shortage of maize from South Africa; these supplies were being blocked by the Rhodesians. Meanwhile, Mugabe's distrust of Nkomo was vindicated when it became known that Nkomo was holding back some of his better-trained troops in Zambia.

Kaunda met Carrington in London, where he was also visited by the leader of the British opposition, James Callaghan. Like Kaunda, Callaghan was adamant that the Patriotic Front must be included in any settlement.

On November 22, Carrington demanded pledges from Mugabe and Nkomo that cross-border raids from Zambia and Mozambique into Rhodesia would cease. Mugabe in turn demanded a two-month truce prior to the election campaign, along with a Commonwealth peacekeeping force of several thousand men. To drum up support for this, he and Nkomo flew to Dar-es-Salaam to meet with the leaders of the Front Line States, all of whom attended except Zambia's Kenneth Kaunda.

Mugabe feared that, although black armies had been given equal status with the whites, the Rhodesian forces might take the opportunity of the cease-fire to herd his forces into detention centers and destroy them "within days." President Machel of Mozambique's reply was, "We hear what you are saying, but we know you will hear us when we say the war must end."[2] Back in London, Mugabe made two further demands. He asked that the white Forces, commanded by General Walls, return to their bases well before his own forces emerged from the bush, and that there be guarantees that South African troops in Rhodesia would be withdrawn, as Mugabe feared they might attack his troops once they were gathered in the assembly camps. Again, there was deadlock over these demands.

A mediator appeared in the shape of Shridath "Sonny" Ramphal, the Commonwealth secretary-general. Mugabe was not satisfied with the following clause in the Constitution: "The British Government will require the governments of countries bordering on Rhodesia to make arrangements to ensure that externally based forces do not enter

Robert Mugabe (left) and Samora Machel (photograph courtesy of Rod Cox).

Rhodesia." Mugabe wanted the words "including South Africa" to be added to this. His request was refused, but the deadlock was finally broken when it was agreed that the Commonwealth monitoring force would be expanded from 600 to 1,200.

In the final plan, the white Rhodesians were to have 47 operational bases for their troops; ZANU-PF, 14. Moreover, none of ZANU-PF's bases would be in the Midlands area between Salisbury and Bulawayo, which was the economic heartland of the Country—where the majority of the whites with their vast farms and settlements were concentrated. Mugabe thought this was unfair and his answer again was "no." Carrington increased pressure by making December 15 the final deadline for agreement.

English-educated Fernando Honwana, aged 28, was a close advisor to Machel and had been sent by him to London as an observer at the conference. He delivered an urgent message to Mugabe from his president: The war was over, and Mugabe must accept the Lancaster House Agreement. Machel realized that his own position might become precarious, for if the talks failed, he was well aware that the Rhodesians had plans to invade Northern Mozambique and deal Mugabe's forces a mortal blow. Mugabe had no choice but to concur.

The Lancaster House Agreement declared that Zimbabwe would be a sovereign republic; that the Constitution would be its supreme law and would prevail over any other law that was inconsistent with it, and that Zimbabwean citizenship would be automatically guaranteed for every person who had been a citizen of Rhodesia immediately before independence.

The president, to be elected by members of Parliament, would be head of state and commander in chief of the defense forces and would hold office for six years, after which he would be eligible for re-election for only one further six-year term of office.

The Senate would consist of 40 members: 10 white, 14 black, 10 to be elected by the Council of Chiefs, and 6 to be nominated by the president on the advice of the prime minister. The House of Assembly (equivalent to the House of Commons) would consist of 100 members: 20 white and 80 black. Any citizen over the age of 18 would be eligible to vote.

The Constitution's Declaration of Rights granted everyone rights to life, to personal liberty, to freedom from slavery and forced labor, to freedom from torture and inhuman treatment, to protection of privacy of home and other property, and to Protection under the law. There would be the right of freedom of conscience, whereby it would be forbidden to interfere with anybody's freedom of thought or religious belief, freedom of expression, freedom of assembly and association, and freedom of movement. There would be protection from discrimination by reason of race, tribe, place of origin, or political opinions.

The Declaration of Rights also stated that there would be freedom from deprivation of property. This was of particular relevance to the white farmers. "Every person will be protected from having his property compulsorily acquired, except when the acquisition is in the interests of defence, public safety, public order, public morality, public health, town and country planning, the development or utilisation of that or other property in such a manner as to promote the public benefit or, in the case of under-utilised land, settlement of land for agricultural purposes. When property is wanted for one of these purposes, its acquisition will be lawful only on condition that the law provides for the prompt payment of adequate compensation and, where the acquisition is contested, that a court order is obtained. A person whose property is so acquired will be guaranteed the right of access to the High Court to determine the amount of compensation." Exception to this rule could be made "during a period of public emergency." "Compensation paid in respect of loss of land to anyone who is a citizen of or ordinarily resident in Zimbabwe (or to a company the majority of whose shareholders are such persons) will, within a reasonable time, be remittable to any country outside Zimbabwe, free from any deduction, tax or charge in respect of its remission."

Annex D of the Agreement dealt with the Pre-Independence Arrangements, and Annex E dealt with the Cease-Fire Arrangements. The Constitution was enacted on December 6, 1979, the signatories being Lord Carrington, Sir Ian Gilmore, Bishop A. T. Muzorewa, R. G Mugabe, J. M. Nkomo and Dr. S. C. Mundawarara of the Muzorewa delegation.[3]

The question now was whether ZANU and ZAPU should fight the election together or separately. Nkomo, who anticipated that he would be the first black prime minister of Rhodesia, believed that they should present a united front, but Mugabe and his central committee thought otherwise and decided to go it alone. The only dissident voice was that of Commander Tongogara, who argued strongly for a joint campaign, with the ZANU and ZAPU armies joining forces.

On the way back from London, Mugabe stopped at Dar-es-Salaam to meet with the leaders of the Front Line States, where he received a setback. President Nyerere made it known that, in his view, a split between ZANU and ZAPU would divide the vote and play into the hands of Bishop Muzorewa.

On Christmas morning, Mugabe arrived back at Maputo in Mozambique, where President Machel and most of his cabinet met him at the airport. Nkomo sent a delegation from Zambia, again urging that the two parties join together. Tongogara agreed, and he also supported Nkomo in his desire to be leader of the proposed new Patriotic Front. However, Tongogara's pleadings were to no avail, and he was dispatched to the guerrilla camps in Mozambique to explain the

Lancaster House Agreement to the guerrilla leaders. However, 100 miles north of Maputo, he was killed in a traffic accident. Although there were suspicions that his death might have been murder, Mugabe seemed genuinely shocked by this event.

Machel had led the FRELIMO forces in the war against the Portuguese, and he then shaped the philosophy of the country after the colonial era when he became president. If Mugabe were to become president of Rhodesia, were there any lessons to be learned from Machel?

Like Mugabe, Machel had been brought up as a Catholic and later became a Marxist. On July 25, 1975 (Independence Day), Mozambique, with a population of 12 million, now found itself with only 2 engineers, 3 agronomists, 5 veterinary surgeons and 36 doctors. The Portuguese had failed to train any native blacks for such professions and, fearing possible FRELIMO atrocities, virtually the entire Portuguese population of 250,000 left the country.

Machel, however, preached racial tolerance. Not only blacks but Asians, coloreds and even whites were members of his party, and in 1980 whites were brought into his cabinet. The vacuum left by the white exodus became obvious. The newly created collective state farms lacked machinery and those with the expertise to run them, and Mozambique was forced to import its basic foodstuffs for the first time. In 1979 the balance of payments deficit was 230 million dollars, a cogent reason for Machel's pressure on Mugabe to make peace with the white Rhodesians, as he could no longer afford to support ZANU guerrillas and refugees in his country.

When the national chain of "people's shops" established by Machel also failed dismally because of owners' lack of marketing expertise, he admitted his mistake. From now on, he said, "the state will create the conditions to support private traders, farmers and industrialists. Private activity has an important role to play in straightening out [the] country."

On January 9, 1980, Machel, at Mugabe's invitation, addressed Mugabe's central committee in Maputo. Urging moderation and pragmatism to the committee's hard-line Marxists, Machel drew a clear distinction between the "lackadaisical, corrupt and cruel" Portuguese colonists[4] and the Rhodesian whites who had much to offer the new

country. In a stark warning, which turned out to be prophetic, he said, "You will face ruin if you force the whites there into precipitate flight."

Machel's words had an impact and were reflected in the party Manifesto, which was produced a few days later. "In working towards the socialist transformation of Zimbabwean society," it said, "a ZANU government will ... recognise historical, social and other existing practical realities of Zimbabwe. ... Hence, while a socialist transformation process will be brought underway in many areas of existing economic sectors, it is recognised that private enterprise will have to continue until circumstances are ripe for socialist change." And as far as different nationalities were concerned, "ZANU wishes to give the fullest assurance to the white community, (and) the Asian and coloured communities that a ZANU government can never in principle or in social or government practice, discriminate against them. Racism, whether practised by blacks or whites, is anathema to the humanitarian philosophy of ZANU."

Then Lord Soames made a request. Mugabe would not be allowed to return to Rhodesia until Mugabe's political opponents, who had been purged from ZANU two years earlier, had been released from jails in Mozambique. Mugabe regarded this as an excuse by the governor to delay his return. Sensing a conspiracy, he declared, that he had "lost every ounce of faith [he] had in the British Government."[5] Nevertheless, prompted by Machel, he agreed to Soames' demand.

After five years in Mozambique, Mugabe and his wife, and 100 or so of his ZANU supporters took the 90-minute flight from Mozambique's Maputo to Salisbury, where tens of thousands of followers were waiting to greet them. The problems they faced were enormous. One million people had been uprooted from their homes and it was now too late in the year for them to sow the crops that could feed them; schools serving half a million children had been closed because of the war; there were scarcely any doctors to serve the rural areas.

At the forthcoming press conference, Mugabe reiterated the theme of ZANU's manifesto. "The State of Zimbabwe must be truly

Opposite: **Mugabe arriving at Beira, Mozambique, in an Air Rhodesia Viscount aircraft, escorted by two MiG fighters (Foreign and Commonwealth Office).**

democratic," he said. "In other words, there must be a complete reversal of the situation where you have equals and unequals, superiors and inferiors, whites and blacks." When he arrived at Highfields township, an estimated 200,000 people sang his praises, held portraits of him aloft, and gave him a five-minute standing ovation.

Although the cease-fire was holding up well, Lord Soames was aware of the vulnerability of his thinly stretched Commonwealth monitoring force, which, in groups of 15 or 20, was sent to await the arrival of the guerrillas into the assembly camps. By mid–January, disturbing reports stated that some of Mugabe's men had broken the terms of the Lancaster House Agreement. Some 3,000 of his men had entered eastern Rhodesia from Mozambique, and of these only 1,000 had arrived at the assembly camps, the remainder were still at large.

Then came another blow to Mugabe's credibility. The eight British advisors, making their interim report on the progress of the election campaign, stated that more than half of the non-white population of Rhodesia was being intimidated by Mugabe's guerrillas and supporters. In five of the country's eight electoral districts, conditions for free and fair elections did not exist. On the other hand, the advisors had found little evidence of intimidation by the 23,000-member army of Bishop Muzorewa—the so-called Rhodesian security force auxiliaries—although there were rumors of this, particularly in the Salisbury township of Harare.

On February 1, 1980, the Mugabes moved into 27 Quorn Avenue, Mount Pleasant, a mainly white suburb of Salisbury, where their own armed bodyguards and a white policeman patrolled the grounds. Lord Soames' message to Mugabe was that the intimidation must stop. "The country [must] get a clean bill of health," he said. "I look to you."[6]

On February 6, a grenade was thrown at Mugabe's house. It exploded harmlessly and there were no casualties. On February 10, however, another attempt was made on his life. Having just attended his second major election rally at Fort Victoria, he was on his way to the local airport to meet the plane that would take him back to Salisbury when a bomb exploded; it had been detonated by remote control by a person standing 100 yards or so away. Five guards in the car following Mugabe's car were injured, and he was badly shaken. Another summons to Government House followed, where Lord Soames demanded again that Mugabe end the intimidation of the electorate.

When two churches in Salisbury were bombed, and an explosion occurred near another church in the black township of Harare, there were accusations and counteraccusations about who had perpetrated these acts. When an issue of the left-wing newspaper *Moto* (which supported the Patriotic Front) appeared containing an attack on Mugabe, suggesting he was "a psychopath suffering from paranoia," the Mambo printing press that produced it was blown up.

At the behest of the governor, General Walls traveled to Mozambique to get President Machel's assurance that he would accept the result of the election, whichever way it went. In return, the governor promised that there would be no military coup in the event of Mugabe's victory. Evidence from the Cease-fire Commission, however, showed that the vast majority of the 207 breaches thus far reported were attributable to Mugabe's forces. One of the advisors stated that "eight black parties are trying to carry out a political campaign, and one is conducting a paramilitary exercise."

Half of the 657 polling stations were mobile and served the remote areas and tribal trust lands. There were special precautions, involving an invisible dye and hand-scanner to prevent anyone from voting more than once. As polling day approached, General Walls called up every available reserve and cancelled all military and police leave. The radio and television station, Parliament and government ministry buildings, and the university, which since December had accommodated ZANLA and ZIPRA officers, were heavily guarded. Summoned again to Government House, Mugabe was asked why, when Nkomo's men had already joined the Rhodesian military to form an integrated army, his men had failed to appear. Finally, General Walls assured Mugabe that there would be no military coup if Mugabe won the election.

The result of the elections would be announced on March 4, 1980. The turnout was massive. Would Mugabe achieve the victory he anticipated?

The Lancaster House Agreement was remarkable more for what was left out of it, rather than for what its 56 pages contained. Of central importance was the future of the white-owned farms, the whites

The signing of the Lancaster House Agreement. Seated, left to right, are Dr. S. C. Mundawarawa, Bishop A. T. Muzorewa, Lord Carrington, Sir I. Gilmour, Bt., Mr. J. M. Nkomo, Mr. R. G. Mugabe (photograph courtesy of Rod Cox).

having the lion's share of and a monopoly interest in the best of the country's farmland: namely the highveld or either side of a line between Salisbury, Bulawayo, and Umtali in the east. Was there a verbal agreement that the sum of $2 billion was what was required to compensate the white farmers fully? Did Britain pledge to raise this sum with the help of other countries? Was it also agreed verbally that for the first ten years there would be no compulsory purchase by the government of white-owned land, but that a willing seller–willing buyer principle would apply?

Mugabe made it clear that he was not wholly satisfied with the terms of the Lancaster House Agreement but was forced to accept them under pressure from the Front Line States. Would he now impose Marxism on the country, at a time when this particular ideology was becoming more and more unfashionable? President

Machel warned him that he risked ruining the economy if he chose to do this.

The forthcoming elections were held in April 1980. Already there were signs of intimidation of the electorate, mainly by Mugabe's ZANU-PF, rather than Nkomo's ZAPU.

7

Victory for Mugabe
and ZANU-PF

At 9 A.M. on March 4, 1980, Sir John Boynton, chairman of the election staff, announced the results. Of the 100 seats in Parliament, Nkomo had gained all 20 seats in Matabeleland, Muzorewa's United African National Congress Party, 3 seats, and ZANU-PF, 57 seats. The remaining 20 seats, had been allocated to whites, including Ian Smith of the Republican Front Party.

Amidst massive cheering, Mugabe, usually demonstrative, stood motionless while Sally embraced everyone around her. As for Nkomo, he was a broken man. "I am the father of Zimbabwe," he said. "What have they done to me?" Of Mugabe, he said, "He was my friend. We fought the war together. We've worked together. We've brought our forces together. And now Robert [Mugabe] has cut me off."[1]

Mugabe's victory caused panic in the white community. Hundreds of houses that were owned by whites were immediately put on the market and white professionals resigned from their jobs in droves. In a television speech, Mugabe sought to allay the whites' fears. "There is no intention on our part to use our majority to victimise the minority. We will ensure there is a place for everyone in this country." For businesses there would be no wholesale nationalization; white civil servants would be guaranteed their jobs and pensions; the rights to property of farmers and householders would be respected; to all people of South Africa there was an offer of peaceful coexistence. "Let us forgive and forget," Mugabe stated. "Let us join hands in a new amity."[2] By the following morning, as a result of this speech, almost all whites withdrew their job resignations and they took hundreds of houses off the market.

The following week, Mugabe fulfilled his promise to make General Walls the supreme commander of the armed forces, and to make two whites members of his first cabinet. He elected David Smith, a former Rhodesia Front minister to be commerce minister, and Dennis Norman, former president of the white farmers' union, to be agriculture minister. Although Nkomo was made the home affairs minister, he realized that his presence in Mugabe's cabinet was purely symbolic. He was, as he put it, nothing more than a "china ornament sitting in the showcase."[3] Nkomo was also aggrieved that his party had been allocated only 4 of the 23 available cabinet seats.

At midnight on April 17, 1980, in the presence of Prince Charles and other world leaders, the British flag was hauled down and replaced by the flag of the new Zimbabwe, with its stripes of green (for the land), gold (for the minerals), red (for blood spilled) and black (for the people). "The wrongs of the past must be forgiven and forgotten," said Mugabe: these words were to have a hollow ring in the years to come.

The Reverend Canaan Banana was to be the first president of the new country (the last country on the African continent to gain independence), and Hector Macdonald became its chief justice. At the independence celebrations in Salisbury's football stadium, Nkomo and his wife maFuyana were excluded from the VIP enclosure and instead, in Nkomo's own words, were "hidden away like something to be scared of."

Of Lord Soames, Mugabe said, "I must admit that I was one of those who originally never trusted him, and yet I have ended up not only implicitly trusting him but also fondly loving him as well." Of his people, Mugabe stated that "if yesterday I fought you as an enemy, today you have become a friend."[4] Her Majesty, the Queen, in a personal message to Mugabe, wrote, "It is a moment for people of all races and all political persuasions to forget the bitterness of the past and to work together to build a better future for their country and for their citizens."[5]

A surprising cordiality apparently existed between Mugabe and Smith, whose government had imprisoned Mugabe for 11 years and had prevented him from attending his son's funeral. Mugabe believed that Smith "appreciated the vital need to retain the confidence of the white people so that they would continue to play their part in building the future of the country."[6] Smith, who continued to run his 6,000-acre farm 200 miles south of Harare, described Mugabe as "a model of reasonableness."[7] At the opening of Parliament on May 15, Mugabe and Smith walked into the debating chamber side by side. Former prime minister Garfield Todd was appointed senator by Mugabe and served in the Senate until his retirement from public life in early 1985.

Mugabe assured the white farmers, who numbered about 6,000 (and owned almost half the land and two-thirds of the most productive land), that he would comply with the verbal agreement reached at Lancaster House that safeguarded their farms from expropriation for a period of ten years. The country's prosperity depended on these farmers, who grew 90 percent of the maize and cotton and almost all of the tobacco, wheat, tea and sugar; these crops accounted for one-third of the country's exports. They also employed 271,000 people, or about one-third of the labor force. Plentiful rainfalls ensured good harvests for two successive years.

Despite Mugabe's assurances, many whites remained apprehensive, particularly about their children's future. Mugabe had already used funds donated by Nigeria to buy the South African company that controlled the majority of Zimbabwe's newspapers; he had sacked their white editors and replaced them with government appointees. Constant propaganda from ZANU-PF was broadcast on radio and television and in the press about "racist whites," and this did nothing to quieten the whites' concerns. In 1980, 17,000 people, one-tenth of the white population, left the country, taking their skills with them.

Britain sent military advisors to help the guerrilla forces integrate with the former Rhodesian army in order to form a new, joint High Command headed by General Walls. This was no easy task. Nkomo's ZIPRA army of some 20,000 men had been recruited mainly from Matabeleland; they spoke in Sindebele and had been trained as a regular force. Mugabe's ZANLA army, on the other hand, which was twice as large, was derived mainly from Shona-speaking areas and had been recruited as a guerrilla force.

To make matters worse, a disillusioned Walls retired from his post as Head of the new joint High Command in July 1980, saying that he had no faith or confidence in Mugabe's leadership. When Walls admitted that he had tried to have the British government declare the election null and void, Mugabe had no choice but to send him into exile.

As Britain began to finance the land-redistribution program, the United States provided Zimbabwe with a three-year aid package worth $225 million; other international donors provided £636 million as a result of the Zimbabwe Conference on Reconstruction and Development (ZIMCORD).

Again, Mugabe offered South Africans the hope of peaceful coexistence. "We are against Apartheid," he said, and although Zimbabweans "have a duty to assist our brothers and sisters," he stated that no nationalist guerrilla bases would be established on Zimbabwean territory.[8] But the guerrillas presented a problem. Although thousands of them wished to remain in the army, only a few hundred could be integrated into the new national force. At the X-ray assembly camp near Mtoko (northeast of Salisbury), discontented guerrillas seized control of the main roads, ambushed vehicles and killed policemen and farmers. In September 1980, when 17,000 guerrillas were moved into temporary accommodation at Chitungwiza, 15 miles from Salisbury, fighting broke out between Mugabe's and Nkomo's men. In November, street battles in Bulawayo between the two rival factions claimed 55 lives with more than 200 people injured. These incidents gave Mugabe legitimate excuses to relieve the guerrilla units of their weapons and to demote Nkomo in January 1981 to the insignificant post of minister in charge of the public service.

Mugabe's government was further embarrassed when Cabinet Minister Tekere, who had spent years in prison with Mugabe, was accused of leading an attack in August 1980 on a farmhouse in which a white farmer was killed. When Tekere was acquitted (after alleging that a plot against Mugabe was being hatched from the farm), whites believed that he had been given a virtual license to kill. Mugabe subsequently dropped Tekere from his cabinet.

Within a year of Mugabe's rise to power, 220,000 Zimbabweans from the refugee camps in Mozambique, Zambia and Botswana had been repatriated, and the maize harvest was good.

Ian Smith, in what was to be his last meeting with Mugabe, expressed his displeasure at Mugabe's support for a one-party state. The South Africans, who now had three avowedly Marxist states—Zimbabwe, Angola and Mozambique—on their northern borders, began recruiting a network of spies and saboteurs inside Zimbabwe, in order to destabilize the regime. They also took control of REN-AMO (the Movement for National Resistance), a guerrilla force that had formerly been established in Mozambique by the white Rhodesians to fight against ZANLA.

In July 1981, the South African Joe Gqabi, chief representative of the ANC in Zimbabwe, was assassinated in Salisbury. A month later, the armory of the Inkomo Military Barracks near Harare exploded. RENAMO forces in Mozambique began to attack communications capacities and the oil pipeline that linked Zimbabwe to the port of Beira in Mozambique.

In August 1981, Mugabe invited North Korean military advisors to Zimbabwe to train a new unit, the 5th Brigade, drawn almost exclusively from former ZANLA troops who were loyal to Mugabe; this brigade would be placed under his personal control. The Shona name for the 5th Brigade was "Gukurahundi" (the wind that sweeps away the chaff before the spring rains) and the sinister reason for its creation would all too soon become apparent.

In December 1981, seven people were killed when a bomb destroyed the ZANU-PF headquarters in central Salisbury. Mugabe believed that "counter-revolutionary elements ... acting in collusion with South Africa" were behind the attacks.[9] In the same month, white MP Wally Stuttaford was arrested, accused of plotting to overthrow the government, and tortured. The government ignored the review tribunal that had declared his imprisonment to be illegal, and also failed to pay the damages awarded to Stuttaford when he sued them.

On February 7, 1982, Mugabe announced that a cache of arms had been discovered on Ascot Farm near Bulawayo in Matabeleland, which belonged to a ZAPU-owned company: one of its directors was Nkomo. This was nothing new, as it was common knowledge that both ZANLA and ZIPRA had cached large quantities of weapons when they returned to Zimbabwe on the cessation of hostilities in 1980. However, Mugabe now alleged that this was evidence of a planned military coup, and, as more farms were raided and more arms dumps were discovered, his language grew more vitriolic. Having Nkomo in the cabinet was like having "a cobra in the house," he said.[10] "The only way to deal effectively with a snake is to strike and destroy its head." Nkomo and his ZAPU allies were promptly dismissed, and his Party's businesses, farms and properties were seized. In the same year, Zimbabwe's capital Salisbury was renamed Harare.

Having been hounded out of the Joint Military Command, Nkomo's increasingly desperate former ZIPRA soldiers (Mugabe called them "dissidents") returned to Matabeleland to rob and murder 600 civilians, including ZANU-PF members, whites (mainly farmers and their families), and foreign tourists. South Africa added fuel to the flames by establishing bases in Northern Transvaal at which to train these former ZIPRA combatants to infiltrate Matabeleland and provoke civil unrest. However, it was not only Nkomo's men who suffered. An estimated 30,000 former ZAPU and ZANU members were unemployed. They had been paid monthly stipends for a time following their demobilization in 1980, but, having failed to find work, most became destitute.

In July 1982, 13 aircraft were sabotaged at Zimbabwe's main air force base at Thornhill, near Gwelo. Several senior air-force officers were arrested, including Air Vice-Marshall Hugh Slatter, and they were tortured until they confessed to involvement in the raid. At their trial in August 1983, Slatter and five of his fellow officers were acquitted and released, only to be immediately re-arrested by the government.

In November 1982, Ian Smith had his passport confiscated because of his "political bad manners and hooliganism." He had criticized Zimbabwe while abroad in Britain and the United States. By 1983, about half of the white population (100,000 people) had left Zimbabwe.

In January 1983, the 5th Brigade was sent into Matabeleland

North to deal with the ex–ZIPRA dissidents. Even though these dissidents were thought to only number a few hundred, Mugabe unleashed barbaric massacres against the entire Ndebele people of that region: once again he had responded to what appeared to be a small, local problem in an entirely disproportionate manner. Rapes, beatings, torture, burnings and deliberate starvation were the order of the day, and 10,000 civilians were killed.

On March 5, 1983, Nkomo's home was attacked. He was away at the time, but his driver and two domestic servants were killed; the Nkomo family were threatened with the same fate if they were to be found. "The dissident party and its dissident father are both destined not only for rejection but for utter destruction as well," said Mugabe. Nkomo fled the country, going first to Botswana and then to Britain.

Bishop Muzorewa, an outspoken critic of Mugabe, compared Mugabe's regime to that of the Ugandan despot Idi Amin. Muzorewa was himself detained from November 1983 until September 1984, when he fled to the United States.

In 1984, following an upsurge of dissident activity in which several white farmers were killed, the 5th Brigade was sent into Matabeleland South to repeat its previous hideous activities. That time, however, the brigade attempted to starve the region's entire population of 400,000, and it flung as many as 8,000 bodies down unused mine shafts, only to have them float to the surface again when the rains came.

In the 1985 parliamentary elections, after Nkomo had returned to the country, ZANU-PF youth brigades (modeled on China's Communist revolutionary Red Guards), did all they could to intimidate the electorate, while the police stood idly by. Nevertheless, Nkomo's ZAPU held all 15 seats in Matabeleland, and Ian Smith also proved that he still had considerable support when his Conservative Alliance of Zimbabwe Party captured 15 of the 20 seats reserved for whites. However, ZANU-PF gained an overall majority of 64 seats.

When the human-rights group Amnesty International described the practice of torture in Zimbabwe as "widespread" and "persistent," Mugabe dismissed its findings as "a heap of lies." He was equally dismissive of a damning report on the same subject by the Catholic Commission for Justice and Peace, and even of the findings of two of his own government commissions.

When Mugabe finally banned ZAPU and jailed its officials, including five of its MPs, Nkomo could withstand the onslaught no longer and on December 22 he signed a "Unity Document" by which Zimbabwe became a one-party state—that party being ZANU-PF. Mugabe had at last achieved the wish that he had first voiced in 1984: "the one party state is more in keeping with African tradition."[11]

Zimbabwe had now joined the Front Line States that were opposed to the white South African apartheid regime. The international community was now anxious to help Zimbabwe, particularly in the fight against the South African–backed RENAMO forces in Mozambique, which were engaged in sporadic incursions along Zimbabwe's eastern border and were disrupting its oil pipeline and trade routes to the east. On September 12, 1986, a bill was introduced in Parliament that ordered the suspension of Ian Smith, who had opposed the imposition of sanctions against the South African regime. Smith resigned as president of the Republican Front (formerly the Rhodesian Front) and retired to his farm at Gwelo. In September 1986, Mugabe was elected as chairman of the Non-Aligned Movement (NAM) of 101 countries. In November 1986, Muzorewa returned to Zimbabwe from the United States.

In 1987, Mugabe chose unilaterally to make various amendments to the Lancaster House Agreement. The post of prime minister was abolished and on December 31, Mugabe was sworn in as executive president. This made him head of state, head of government and commander-in-chief of the defense forces. He now had the power to dissolve Parliament and declare martial law; to control all senior posts in the police, civil service and military; and to run for as many terms of office as he wished. Also, since independence, he had renewed the state of emergency every six months, giving the government authority to detain people without trial, even after they had been acquitted by the courts. Mugabe abolished the clause that reserved 20 of the 100 parliamentary seats for whites, and this, together with the merging of ZANU-PF with ZAPU, reduced the strength of his opposition to a single seat: that of the tiny ZANU-Ndonga party (founded by the Reverend Sithole when he had been forced out of ZANU-PF). At that point, only 40,000 families had been resettled out of an intended target, set by Mugabe when he came to power in 1980, of 160,000.

When Sally, who was well respected for her work with children's charities, was diagnosed with a kidney disease, Mugabe was frank about his own intentions. "I knew the life of my first wife was going to be short," he said, "so I knew how to prepare for life after her."[12] In 1987, he embarked on a clandestine affair with Grace Marufu, one of his office secretaries, who was 40 years his junior and married with a son. "I wanted children," said Mugabe, "and this is how I thought I could get them." In 1988, Mugabe declared amnesty for the soldiers of the infamous 5th Brigade (so they were safe from prosecution), and in the same year, Grace had her first child by Mugabe, Bona, who was named after his mother.

In September 1988, Mugabe was awarded the Africa Prize for "Leadership for the Sustainable End of Hunger," by the U.S.-based Hunger Project. (This was ironic, as Mugabe was to embark on a course of action that would all but destroy his country's agricultural base.) The $100,000 prize money was allegedly used to launch a National Agricultural Scholarship Fund.

Even Edgar Tekere, once Mugabe's staunchest friend, had become an outspoken critic of his policies. "A new class of masters" had emerged, Tekere said, and had "hijacked the revolution." "I fear we are heading towards a dictatorship. ... Democracy in Zimbabwe is in intensive care and the leadership has decayed."[13] In April 1989, Tekere launched a new party, the Zimbabwe Unity Movement (ZUM), and gained immediate support from the black townships of Harare, Bulawayo, Mutare (formerly Umtali), and from the students of the university. However, he damned himself in Mugabe's eyes by joining forces with the all-white Conservative Alliance of Zimbabwe, which was the direct descendant of the Rhodesia Front. Mugabe's response was predictable, and the ZUM was subjected to the same intimidation and brutality that ZANU had previously suffered. In Gweru (formerly Gwelo), the authorities went so far as to alter the electoral boundaries in order to give ZANU-PF a better chance.

When Tekere challenged Mugabe for the presidency in 1990, he acquired only 17 percent of the votes following widespread intimidation by Mugabe's supporters; after this, Tekere's party simply disappeared and he retired in poverty. Mugabe then accused the Reverend

Sithole of attempting to assassinate him by blowing up the presidential car, referring to the February 1980 grenade incident.

In 1990, the year that Nelson Mandela was released from prison in South Africa, Grace Marufu bore Mugabe a second child, Robert. Mugabe continued to attend Sunday Mass at Harare's Catholic Cathedral. Being the son of a God-fearing mother (and a Roman Catholic bound by the ten commandments), Mugabe must have felt much guilt about his adulterous relationship.

Mugabe took further steps to consolidate his already overwhelming parliamentary strength by increasing the number of members to 150, of which only 120 could be elected by the general public. Of the remainder, 20 would be appointed by the president and 10 would be chiefs—to be elected by a council of chiefs whose appointments Mugabe controlled.

For the 1990 parliamentary election, candidates came from Mugabe's ZANU-PF Party, Bishop Muzorewa's United Parties (an amalgamation of Muzorewa's former United African National Council, and the Forum Party founded in 1993), the Reverend Sithole's ZANU-Ndonga Party, Austin Chakaodza's Popular Democratic Front, Edgar Tekere's Zimbabwe Unity Movement and Margaret Donga's Independent Party. As expected, Mugabe won 117 of the 120 contested seats. However, owing to reservations within ZANU-PF, and the news that neighboring Mozambique had abandoned its Marxist aspirations in favor of a multiparty system, Mugabe was forced to postpone his plans for a one-party state. In 1991, ZANU-PF formerly deleted all references to "Marxist-Leninism" and "scientific socialism" from its Constitution.

After his overwhelming victory in the 1990 election, Mugabe adopted a humble demeanor. Despite this, however, he continued to humiliate and isolate his main rival Nkomo: first by not inviting him and his wife to the VIP enclosure for the independence celebrations, and then by offering Nkomo a post in the cabinet, which was, in effect, purely symbolic.

Mugabe went even further, and sent the 5th Brigade into Matabeleland again to quell the unrest there. This unrest, however, was caused principally by the fact that no provisions had been made for the thousands of former ZIPRA troops who had been discharged from the armed services and were destitute. The scale of military activity by ZANU-PF was quite disproportionate to the size of the problem, and their widespread atrocities against Nkomo's Ndebele people were universally condemned.

In 1987 when Mugabe was sworn in as executive president of Zimbabwe, he became a virtual dictator. However, power had not been his sole objective. By continuing to persecute Nkomo and his people long after the election had been fought and won, Mugabe showed that what he actually wanted was total control.

8

The Land Question

In 1981, the second year of Mugabe's premiership, the economy of Zimbabwe was booming, and the most important economic activity—the one on which the livelihoods of four-fifths of the population depended—was agriculture.

The land supported 5 million cattle, 386,000 sheep, 1,335,000 goats and 146,000 pigs. In 1981, 2 million tons of maize was produced, more than double the country's requirements and the surplus was exported. In 1981–82, 89 million kilograms of tobacco was produced, of which 96 percent was exported.[1] Sadly, within two decades, these industries, together with the mining and tourism economies, would be destroyed.

The question of who had a rightful claim to the ownership of the land was one that had bedeviled the country for generations. At Independence in 1980, 39 percent of the land was owned by 6,000 white farmers, as compared to 4 percent held by 8,000 black farmers. Of the remaining land, 41 percent was communal land inhabited by 4 million people—overwhelmingly black—with national parks and forests making up the final 16 percent. (Under the Communal Land Act of 1981, tribal trust lands became communal areas, no longer administered by local paramount chiefs, but by local authorities.) To Mugabe, the issue was a simple one: Rhodes and his pioneers had stolen the land from the blacks in the late nineteenth century; the blacks had every right to regain what was originally theirs. The Land Acquisition Act of 1985, drafted in accordance with the Lancaster House Agreement, gave the government the first right of purchase of white farms for resettlement by blacks.

In the ten years since Independence, about 8.5 million acres of land had been purchased from the whites by mutual consent, under the terms of the Lancaster House Agreement, and paid for by the United Kingdom with £44 million in aid. However, although 416,000 blacks had been resettled on this land, this fell short of the government's target of over 1 million. Also, contrary to expectation, many of these resettled families soon returned home, in the absence of financial or material help or the technical expertise to enable them to make a success of an industry that had taken over a century to create. MPs, civil servants, and police and military officials were not slow to benefit from this and by 1990, 8 percent of commercial farmland was owned by them: although they too lacked the wherewithal to make the land productive.

Mugabe was in a dilemma. On one hand, he was expected to fulfill the expectations of those who had helped him and who had fought for him in the struggle by rewarding them with land owned by the white farmers; on the other hand, insufficient funds were available for the purchase of this land, even if the whites involved wished to sell it. What if Mugabe chose to take the whites' land by force? As one British diplomat put it, "if he [Mugabe] takes too much away from the whites, they will leave, but if he gives too little to the blacks, they will revolt."[2]

In December 1990, the Constitution was amended to empower the government to confiscate land at a price it determined was fair, and the government could deny any right of appeal to the court in the event that the compensation was considered unfair by the white farmer concerned. In this way the government aimed to acquire some 13 million acres, or almost half of the remaining white-owned land. Enoch Dumbutshena, Zimbabwe's first black chief justice, denounced this action, saying that "it flies in the face of all accepted norms of modern society."[3]

The Commercial Farmers' Union organized a meeting between 4,000 white farmers and the Zimbabwean minister of agriculture. At this meeting, however, the minister said that the subject was not negotiable. Britain, the United States, the IMF, and the World Bank warned that, unless the farmers were guaranteed fair compensation, crucial aid packages would not be forthcoming. This prompted the government of Zimbabwe to remove the clause that banned a white farmer's right to appeal in the event that he considered his compensation to be unfair. Peace reigned—for the moment at least.

Mugabe had begun a massive expansion of the educational system, which in two decades would see a tenfold increase in schools and pupils; literacy rates would rise from 62 percent to 82 percent of the population. At the same time, child immunization rates would rise from 25 percent to 90 percent. However, despite these successes and Mugabe's possession of two degrees in economics, the economy went into sharp decline, and his controls over prices, dividends and exchange rates caused foreign investment virtually to cease. A reform package put together by the IMF was largely ignored, and the end result was that fit, healthy and well-educated young people were being released into a society where there were no jobs, except perhaps in teaching.

In 1991, Mugabe accepted the Structural Adjustment Program proposed by the IMF and agreed to economic reforms, one of which was to encourage a free market. That October, he hosted the Summit Conference of Commonwealth leaders, and he signed the Harare Declaration of Democratic Principles, which committed Zimbabwe to full political freedom. However, in the words of Alois Mangwenda, chairman of the parliamentary public accounts committee, "corruption" had become pervasive, and civil servants, "venal and rapacious."[4] One major beneficiary of these reforms was Mugabe's nephew, Leo, the son of his sister Sabina, who received $190,000 for ensuring that a Cypriot firm, Air Harbour Technologies (AHT), obtain the contract to build Harare's new $80 million airport terminal building.

When Sally died in 1992, Mugabe lost someone who had been a moderating influence on his behavior. He became more and more remote from reality, without close friends; as president, he was not even obliged to attend Parliament and answer questions on government policy. In March 1992, he became chairman of the Front Line States.

The Land Acquisition Act of 1992 was designed to acquire more land for blacks who resided in congested areas that were adversely affected by inadequate rainfall. This act applied to derelict land, under-utilized land, land owned by absentee landlords, land belonging to farmers with more than one farm or with overly large farms, and land adjacent to communal areas. Should the landowner not agree to the price offered by the acquiring authority, he could appeal to the court. This Act went beyond what had been agreed at Lancaster House. When a small group of farmers challenged the legality of the Land Acquisition Act, this was Mugabe's angry response: "We will not brook any decision by any court [to prevent us] from acquiring any land."[5]

In July 1992 the government, without warning and despite the previous agreement with the CFU, designated 13 farms in the Mutare (formerly Umtali) district for acquisition but then decided for reasons known only to itself to "undesignate" seven of them. In 1993, another 70 farms were designated, including those of Ndabaningi Sithole (ZANU's first leader prior to Mugabe) and James Chikerema, another of Mugabe's political opponents. The meaning was clear. It was revenge—taken against rivals who no longer posed a credible threat.

In April 1994, the month the ANC won the South African elections and Nelson Mandela was elected president, there was a scandal in Zimbabwe over these land issues. An independent newspaper reported that a 3,000-acre farm had been purchased by the government despite the white owner's objections, on the pretext that it was to be used for the resettlement of 33 homeless peasants. In fact, however, it was leased to Witness Mangwende, former minister of agriculture and then minister of education, as a reward for his promotion of the Land Acquisition Act. Further investigations revealed numerous other resettlement scandals in which the beneficiaries were invariably high-ranking officials who were loyal to Mugabe.

In the face of popular indignation, Mugabe agreed to cancel 72 farm leases, but John Major's British conservative government had seen enough. Having provided £44 million for land resettlement to Zimbabwe since Independence, Britain ceased all such further payments. Aid for development, however, was continued.

Mugabe found himself backed into a corner. For all his anti-white posturing, he knew that it was the white farmers who not only produced most of the country's food, but who also employed 300,000 black workers and their families. In a land where the standard of living for the majority was falling rapidly, what could he offer to fulfill the expectations of increasingly disillusioned people and to persuade them that ZANU-PF still represented the party of change and progress? The answer was nothing, apart from the prospect of taking over the white farmers' land; as there was no money available to enable him to do this, he had to find ways to simply confiscate it.

Margaret Dongo had joined ZANU at the age of 15 and then crossed to Mozambique in 1975 (the same year as Mugabe) to work as a medical assistant. She was a founding member of the War Veterans' Association, and she became a member of ZANU-PF's central committee and of its women's league. Disillusioned with ZANU-PF, which expelled her from its membership, she decided to run in the forthcoming April 1995 election as an independent candidate. "I would have died for Mugabe," she said. "But once [his government] got their farms, houses and limos, they forgot about the people who put them there." In the election, ZANU-PF again won an overwhelming victory, capturing 118 of the 120 seats.[6]

In October 1995, the Reverend Sithole was arrested and charged with arms possession, terrorism, and conspiracy to murder President Mugabe (there had been an attack on Mugabe's motorcade on August 4); on February 17, 1996, he was remanded in prison and then released on bail of Z$100,000. In December 1997, two years after his arrest, Sithole was sentenced to two months' imprisonment for conspiring to murder Mugabe, but he was released pending an appeal. Sithole would pass away three years later, while in the United States.

In 1996, when Muzorewa and Sithole challenged Mugabe for the Presidency—in an election that everybody knew to be a sham— Mugabe won with 92.7 percent of the vote. However, turnout was a mere 31.7 percent: amongst the disillusioned electorate of Bulawayo, a mere 16 percent.

Margaret Dongo could not believe that she had not achieved victory in the Harare South constituency, where she had massive support; when both the registrar-general and the electoral commission refused to investigate, she appealed to the High Court, which found irregularities in the proceedings and ordered that another election be held the following November: that time she won.

Rather than accept the austerity measures urged on him by the World Bank and the IMF, Mugabe increased the size of his cabinet from 29 to 42 ministers, and the enlarged cabinet in turn awarded Mugabe and all MPs pay raises of 133 percent, while at the same time It cut the health budget by 43 percent.

On August 17, 1996, Mugabe married Grace Marufu in the tiny church at Katuma Mission where he had lived as a boy. Archbishop Patrick Chakaipa, head of the Catholic Church, officiated, albeit Reluctantly. The best man was Joachim Chissano, president of Mozambique, and President Nelson Mandela of South Africa was a guest of honor. Unlike Sally, Grace showed little interest in charitable causes: she preferred a life of luxury and was not averse to feathering her nest by speculating on the housing market at the government's expense.

When he married Grace, Mugabe expected that she, being an heiress, would bring with her a considerable dowry. When her family refused to countenance such an idea, Mugabe angrily smashed every window in his official residence, the State House—demonstrating once again his intolerance to opposition, wherever it might come from.

The organization of Front Line States had become the Southern African Development Community (SADC), and in June 1996 Mugabe was elected chairman of its defense wing. This would give him further opportunities to perform on an international stage. That December, Brigadier Gibson Mashingaidze attended the funeral of impoverished war veteran Mukoma Musa, for whom the he had paid Z$1,000 out of his own pocket in order to give Musa a decent burial. "Some people now have ten farms to their names and luxury yachts, and have developed fat stomachs," said the Brigadier bitterly, "when ex-combatants like Comrade Musa lived in abject poverty. Is this the ZANU-PF I trusted with my life? Is this the same party which promised to care for us in our old age? To the majority of Zimbabweans, I say our party, which I believe is still a great party, has abandoned us."

In 1997 Grace bore Mugabe a second son, Chatunga. In March the government was forced to suspend payments from the War

Veterans' Compensation Fund as the Z450 million (equivalent to U.S. $40 million) allocated for that year had been used up after only eight months. Pilfering by senior politicians and officials was suspected. When Margaret Dongo tabled a motion in Parliament, asking the auditor-general to investigate the disappearance of the funds, more than 100 other MPs supported her, forcing Mugabe to appoint a commission of enquiry under High Court Judge Godfrey Chidyausiku to look into the matter.

A vivid example of such misappropriation of funds was demonstrated by the executive mayor of Harare, Solomon Tawengwa, who had come to office in 1995. He was building himself a new mayoral mansion at a cost of Z$65 million, while the infrastructure of his city—its public health facilities, sanitation, hospitals and transport—was sinking into decrepitude.

Tony Blair's Labour Party came to power in Britain on May 2, 1997, but the problem of Zimbabwe remained unresolved. The two countries mainly disagreed over the interpretation of the Lancaster House Agreement of 1979. Mugabe believed that Britain should pay for land reform without preconditions; the previous British conservative government had contributed £44 million, with further payments made after that until 1995. Mugabe was anxious for these payments to be restored. Britain, however, insisted on certain conditions: one was that some of the money should go toward helping the country's poorest people. The stalemate continued.

In July 1997, one month after Mugabe had assumed the chairmanship of the Organization of African Unity, impoverished war veterans demonstrated for three days on the streets of Harare, besieging his office and disrupting a conference for American investors that he was hosting; on Heroes Day (August 11), they forced him to cut short a speech he was making by jeering and drumming. Yet another scandal was about to rock the government.

Under the terms of the War Victims' Compensation Act, former combatants were entitled to make claims for injuries sustained during the war. Judge Chidyausiku discovered that the system had been grossly abused. Chenjerai Hitler Hunzvi, leader of the war veterans and assessor of claims, had awarded himself Z$517,536 for "impaired hearing" and "sciatic pains of the thigh." Not to be outdone, the aptly named Reward Marufu, Mugabe's brother-in-law, was awarded Z$822,668 for "a scar on his left knee," and "ulcers"! Numerous other high-ranking officials were paid similar amounts for conditions such as "skin allergy," "polyarthritis," "mental stress disorder," and so forth.[7] Although Margaret Dongo successfully called upon the auditor-general to investigate the matter, no one was ever brought to account for the fraud, nor was any of the money ever reclaimed.

The war veterans were outraged at the fact that they had received no reward for putting Mugabe in power, and that former soldiers in the Rhodesian army received pensions, while they received nothing. In August 1997, with the unemployment rate approaching 50 percent, Mugabe agreed to pay them the gratuities and pensions that they demanded. Each war veteran was granted a lump sum of Z$50,000 and a monthly payment of Z$2,000: the bill totalling Z$4.2 billion (over £260 million). Veterans would also be given land, free education and free healthcare in another package costing Z$4 billion. Because of this huge drain on a bankrupt economy, the Zimbabwean dollar slumped.

When British Prime Minister Blair met Mugabe briefly at the Commonwealth summit in Edinburgh in October 1997, the atmosphere of the meeting was decidedly frosty. In November, Clare Short, Britain's international development secretary, went a step further when she wrote to Zimbabwe's agriculture minister to say "I should make it clear that we do not accept that Britain has a special responsibility to meet the cost of land purchase in Zimbabwe."[8] Britain now appeared to have washed its hands of the land problem altogether.

That same month, Mugabe announced that 1,503 white-owned farms were to be compulsorily seized; this number represented roughly 45 percent of the total land held by Zimbabwe's 4,500 commercial farmers. Without funds this plan was not implemented, but the result of Mugabe's announcement was twofold. First, the stock market plummeted, and then the British government restated its position. It was willing to help, but only if land redistribution would alleviate the burdens of the poor.

Morgan Tsvangirai, 47 years old, was a miner who had become vice-president of the Zimbabwe Mine Workers' Union. A former supporter of ZANU-PF, he had obtained a diploma in productivity at Cresta College in Nottingham, England, at a time when union leader Arthur Scargill was leading his mineworkers into battle on the picket lines against the government. On his return to Zimbabwe in 1988, Tsvangirai was appointed secretary-general of the Zimbabwe Congress of Trade Unions (ZCTU), an organization that represented 27 unions—whose 400,000 members made up one-third of the country's workforce. He was instrumental in organizing the General Strike of December 1997 to protest the raising of taxes by Mugabe to cover the cost of paying war veterans.

Mugabe reacted with predictable brutality. Tsvangirai was severely beaten; He was rescued in the nick of time by his security guards when his attackers attempted to throw him out of the window of his tenth-floor office. However, when the unpopular new tax scheme was withdrawn, the Reserve Bank simply printed more money to make good the deficit.

In January 1998, there were food riots in the black townships of Harare. The army was deployed, but several people were killed and hundreds injured.

During the 1990s, Mugabe visited—along with his large retinue—151 foreign countries. In August 1998 he used his influence as chairman of SADC's defense wing to persuade Namibia and Angola to join him in coming to the aid of President Laurent Kabila, whose forces had ousted the autocratic and oppressive regime of President Sese Mobutu in the Democratic Republic of Congo. Kabila's forces were coming under attack from rebels in the east of the country, where a civil war had been raging since August 1988.

Zimbabwe initially sent 3,000 troops, together with armored vehicles and support aircraft; this figure soon rose to 11,000, at a cost to Mugabe's impoverished country of $1 million per day. In October 1998, it was rumored that heavy defeats had been inflicted on the Zimbabwean troops by the rebels and that many of them had been captured as prisoners.

In return, Kabila offered mining and timber concessions to Zimbabwe, and also preferential trade rates for diamonds, cobalt and other minerals. Special allowances were paid to Zimbabwean soldiers serving in the Congo, but as usual it was Zimbabwe's ruling elite who most benefited from new opportunites to trade in arms, food and consumer goods.

In September 1998 the International Donors' Conference on Land Reform in Zimbabwe was held in Harare; the IMF, the World Bank, the European Union and representatives of 23 foreign governments and international organizations attended: they were all potential donors of funds. The government of Zimbabwe estimated that $1.1 billion would be required to cover the cost of land acquisition and development, infrastructure and services (including road construction, water, first crop tillage, schools and clinics), farmer support and credit facilities. A resettlement program was agreed to run over two years and involve 118 farms already offered for sale by their white owners. It would be overseen by a technical support unit financed by the United Nations. This all sounded very good, but, as so often was the case, nothing came of it. Instead, two months later, a defiant Mugabe announced that 841 white-owned farms would be seized.

In the 19 years since Independence, the white farmers had parted with 30 percent of their total landholdings, for which compensation had been paid out of the £44 million donated by Britain. However, 21 percent of the land still remained in the hands of 4,000 members of the white-dominated Commercial Farmers' Union. So who were the black beneficiaries of land reform, and what did they do with the farms they acquired?

For the poor people—whose numbers were legion—Mugabe believed in the ideology of Chinese-style socialism. "Collectives" would be created, where people with no title to the land would live in villages and be expected to grow food for the mutual benefit of themselves and their comrades. This was despite the fact that other socialist countries, including China, were beginning to embrace the idea of a free-market economy. What happened was that the settlers were conveyed to their new farms, only to find the water supply in disrepair through neglect or vandalism; the absence of seed, fertilizer, livestock, supervision or financial backing left them with no alternative but to loot what they could, to hunt down any wild animals for their meat, and to quietly return from whence they had come. The farms then fell into dereliction.

For Mugabe's party officials, members of the armed forces, war veterans' leaders, High Court judges, family and friends, the Commercial Farm Resettlement Scheme was established whereby they could lease farms from the government. It went without saying that anyone withdrawing support for ZANU-PF would have his lease revoked immediately. Other beneficiaries were five reporters on the *Herald* newspaper—the mouthpiece for ZANU-PF.

On January 10, 1999, the *Standard* Sunday independent newspaper reported that 23 officers and soldiers had been arrested for plotting a military coup. Mugabe declared this story to be "traitorous" and it was now the press' turn to feel his wrath. The paper's editor, Mark Chavunduka, and its reporter, Ray Choto, both of whom were black, were arrested and tortured by the army; the army ignored three orders from the High Court that they be released. Mugabe then appeared on television and spoke of "the acts of some white persons of British extraction who have been planted in our midst to undertake acts of sabotage aimed at affecting the loyalty not just of people in general but also that of the vital arm of Government like the army, so that these can turn against the legitimate Government of this country"[9] and included all white Zimbabweans in his list of subversive elements. He saw the conflict purely in terms of black versus white or, in other words, in racist terms.

On January 21, 1999, the two journalists from the *Standard* were charged in a magistrate's court, under the Law and Order (Maintenance) Act, with publishing false reports "likely to cause alarm, fear or despondency to the public," and were then released on bail. When a group of 150 lawyers and human-rights protestors demonstrated outside Parliament, their gathering was brutally dispersed by the police.

The most scathing condemnation of Mugabe's transgressions against the rule of law came in a letter to him from three Supreme Court judges (two black and one white), with an endorsement from another two judges who were abroad at the time. Mugabe loftily pronounced this letter to be, "an outrageous and deliberate piece of impudence."[10] The judiciary had no right to give "instructions" to the president.

The charges against the journalists, however, were dismissed by the 25 judges of the Supreme Court, 17 of whom were non-white. The Court was adamant that individual human rights be upheld. However, a claim for damages by the journalists against the police, who had handed them over to the army, failed when the commissioner of police refused to take any action.

In February 1999, the Zimbabwean Electricity Supply Authority (ZESA) became insolvent due to "entrenched corruption" and excessive government controls. The state oil company, NOCZIM, having been defrauded by its managers of $150 million over five years, ran out of money to pay for oil imports. Supplies were cut off and this caused crippling fuel shortages. People were told that they could call for emergency services, but in turn they must supply emergency vehicles with adequate fuel for the return journey.

Trade union leader Tsvangirai organized a series of protest strikes aimed at forcing the government to change its ways, whereupon Mugabe issued a decree under the Presidential Powers (Temporary Measures) Act, banning national strikes for six months. Aware that Tsvangirai was seeking public support for a new Constitution, the government set up its own commission to draft a new Constitution to be placed before the electorate in a referendum. Three-quarters of the commission's 400 members (which included all 147 MPs) would be ZANU-PF members, and the remaining one-quarter would be independent.

The IMF now lost patience with Zimbabwe's expensive intervention in the Congo, land redistribution policy, and economic failures and therefore decided to withhold funds. Mugabe responded by saying that the IMF was "bent on stifling development in the Third World."[11] As western governments and the World Bank followed suit in challenging Zimbabwe, Britain's response was also unsupportive. "We will not support corrupt governments ... subsidise economic mismanagement ... [or] fund repression or bankroll dictatorship,"[12] said British Minister of State Peter Hain. Britain had been prepared to offer £36 million for the alleviation of poverty but only if fundamental changes were made, including economic reforms. On June 30, 1999, Joshua Nkomo died in hospital in Harare of cancer of the prostate gland.

In practice, the willingness of white farmers to sell had been overestimated. Land was not offered to the government in sufficient amounts to satisfy the aspirations of land-hungry blacks living in

The Rt. Hon. Peter Hain

overcrowded areas, and what little land that was offered was of poor quality, and in areas of inadequate rainfall. Finally, through lack of funds, the government was unable to offer the market price anyway.

Even when farms were repossessed, the occupancy rate after a year was less than 50 percent. Although Mugabe had economics degrees, no amount of learning could compensate for hands-on experience where farming was concerned: those farms that had been resettled quickly became unproductive.

Sally's moderating influence on Mugabe's behavior was lost when she died in 1992. Increasingly, Mugabe behaved like an autocrat, ignoring the advice of the IMF, the World Bank and potential investor-countries, and he deluded himself that he could go it alone. Court rulings by judges (who were predominantly black) were ignored, and pressmen were assaulted, tortured and vilified when they dared to say a word against him.

9

The Movement for Democratic Change

On September 11, 1999, the people of Zimbabwe found a new voice when the Movement for Democratic Change was launched before a crowd of 15,000 people at the Rufaro Football Stadium where, 19 years before, Zimbabwe's Independence Day celebrations had been held. The Movement's leader, Morgan Tsvangirai of the Zimbabwe Congress of Trade Unions, had "flexed his muscles" in the General Strikes of 1997 and 1998. The June 2000 elections would be a chance for his supporters to demonstrate their opposition to Mugabe.

Mugabe, to whom the whole concept of opposition was anathema, reacted characteristically. Instead of welcoming the MDC into the democratic process, he dismissed the new party as being a front for whites, and he felt that Tsvangirai and his supporters were traitors to their country. He also believed that Britain, through the MDC, intended to re-colonize Zimbabwe. In reality Britain was divesting itself of colonies (both in Africa and elsewhere as quickly as was conveniently possible). It seems that Mugabe was creating another excuse for attacking the new party?

When Peter Hain, Britain's minister of state at the Foreign Office, met Mugabe in October 1999, there were hopes of a reconciliation between the two countries. The day after the meeting, however, an

Morgan Tsvangirai visiting the Harare Hospital on March 5, 2002 (photograph courtesy of the Movement for Democratic Change Zimbabwe).

unexpected incident took place. As Mugabe's motor cavalcade left his hotel at Buckingham Gate for a shopping expedition to Harrods, gay rights activists surrounded his car and one of them, Peter Tatchell, flung open the door of the car, grabbed him by the arm and shouted, "President Mugabe, you are under arrest for torture!" Tatchell then berated him over the torture of Choto and Chavunduka, the two Zimbabwean journalists. Mugabe, who was prejudiced against homosexuals, saw this occurrence not as a relatively peaceful protest by someone living in a country that tolerated free speech; rather he saw it as part of a conspiracy by Prime Minister Blair to use "gay gangsters" to threaten him.

The constitutional commission set up by Mugabe proposed in November 1999 that "the former colonial power [Britain] has an obligation to pay compensation for agricultural land compulsorily acquired [from whites by Mugabe] for resettlement [by blacks]," and that, in the event of no payments being forthcoming, the government of Zimbabwe "had no obligation to pay" such compensation (to white farmers). Further commissions would be set up to consider reforms to public finances, law and order, electoral procedure and government relations with the media, but under the proposed new Constitution Mugabe would be allowed to hold office for another ten years. This was in flagrant violation of the Lancaster House Agreement.

By December 1999, with Zimbabwe having no foreign exchange reserves left, the IMF withdrew all support. As far as international creditors were concerned, the country was now considered to be a bad risk and no further loans were forthcoming: supplies of gasoline quickly ran out. Seeking a scapegoat for this disaster, Mugabe blamed the white farmers. "We know we bought adequate supplies of fuel," he said, "but they [the farmers] bought all of it in large drums and hid them on their farms." In January 2000, with inflation running at 58.5 percent, basic foodstuffs became unaffordable for the majority of the population; Mugabe decided to hold a referendum.

The electorate was asked to vote on whether Mugabe should be permitted to retain the powers of the presidency and run for another two five-year terms of office. There was also a clause that transferred responsibility for paying for land reform from Zimbabwe to Britain. The "Vote Yes" campaign was vigorously sponsored by Mugabe, to the extent that television advertisements produced by the "Vote No" campaigners were banned from broadcast on the state-run Zimbabwe Broadcasting Company (ZBC). Three of the "No" campaigners' advertisements were broadcast, however, but only after intervention by the High Court. The referendum election took place in February 2000. Although the turnout was only 25 percent, the "No" campaign won with 54.7 percent of the vote.

Mugabe appeared to be unphased by these unexpected results, saying to the people, "The world now knows Zimbabwe as a country where opposing views and opinions can be found alongside each other peacefully. Let us all, winners and losers, accept the referendum verdict and start planning our way for the future."[1] But, as always, Mugabe and ZANU-PF looked for a scapegoat. Information Minister Chen Chimutengwende blamed election results on "the Rhodesians, neo-colonialists, and other retrogressive forces" and political spokes-man Jonathan Moyo, who had organized the "Yes" campaign, claimed that victory had come about unfairly because white voters had entered the country in large numbers from South Africa, in order to vote in the referendum.

In the 20 years since Independence, only 10 percent of arable land had passed legally from white to black owners, yet some 6,000 white farmers still held almost half the land. Meanwhile, the number of poor people requiring land rose to 500,000.

Early in 2000, the patience of the Zimbabwe Liberation War Veterans' Association finally ended, and, on February 26 there were large-scale invasions of white-owned farms. Their leader, Chenjerai Hunzvi, admitted that ZANU-PF had given him $2 million for his services, which they hoped would deter whites from campaigning against Mugabe.

On March 1, 2000, the vice-president of Zimbabwe, Joseph Msika, met with British High Commissioner Peter Longworth and told him, "We're fed up with you British, and we're going to go our own way." Msika declared that Britain was "interfering with our polit-ical process and organising the MDC." As for the referendum's "No" vote, Msika claimed that it was "organised by you British and the white farmers." However, it was not only the white farmers who were to endure the forthcoming onslaught of beatings, torture and murder at the hands of the members of the War Veterans' Association. Their black farm laborers were to be "re-educated" and any with MDC sym-pathies were to expect no mercy. For their services, ZANU-PF paid the war veterans Z$20 million (about £330,000); a squatter would earn about Z$50 (or 80 pence) per day spent occupying a white farm.

When Home Affairs Minister Dumiso Dabengwa announced that he had "decided to instruct the war veterans to withdraw from the farms with immediate effect,"[2] he was overruled by the increas-ingly powerful Hunzvi. By March 6, 250 white farms were occupied illegally. By March 8, about 400 farms had been invaded, as squatters had been transported to them in government and army trucks; as usual, the police stood idly by, claiming it was a political issue.

Seeking revenge for the Tatchell incident in London, Mugabe

ordered customs officials at Harare's airport to search a British diplomatic bag imported by the British High Commission. This was in breach of international law. All that was found was routine electronic equipment used for preventing eavesdroppers from listening in on private conversations. However, Mugabe's actions infuriated the British and provoked fierce rhetoric from Hain, who in turn infuriated Mugabe by saying that the bag search was "not the act of a civilised country." The British government did not wish to inflame Mugabe's anger further against the white population, but it was nevertheless anxious to show its displeasure. It therefore refused to supply any more free Land Rovers and froze development aid, apart from money directed to charities.

On March 10, Mugabe made a speech in which he said, "We want the whites to learn that the land belongs to the Zimbabweans." This unequivocal statement showed that, despite the fact that the vast majority of white farmers possessed Zimbabwean passports, Mugabe did not regard the whites as citizens of the country. ZANU-PF, and in particular its militant youth group, saw this as a license to perpetrate a reign of terror; their first victim was 16-year-old Edwin Gomo, who was killed on his way to an MDC rally.

On March 17, High Court Judge Justice Paddington Garwe declared that "every occupation of any property ... is hereby declared unlawful," and that "all persons who have taken up the occupation of any commercial farm ... shall vacate that land within 24 hours of the making of this Order." This order was ignored by the government; despite the judge's vehemence, the number of occupied farms rose until, by the end of March, it stood at 800.[3]

On April 1, 2000, the National Constitutional Assembly—an alliance of church and civic groups, human-rights activists, lawyers and journalists—organized a "March for Peace" through the center of Harare. Over 7,000 people, including blacks and whites of all classes, expressed their opposition to political intimidation and to the invasions of the farms. This "March for Peace" was a peaceful demonstration, until about 200 war veterans, who had assembled at ZANU-PF headquarters under Hunzvi' supervision, attacked and savagely beat the marchers with clubs and iron bars in full view of the riot police who failed to intervene. After this "triumph," ZANU-PF escalated its campaign of intimidation and occupation, by committing acts of unspeakable savagery and indoctrinating the masses using techniques taught to them by Mugabe's Chinese instructors—techniques similar to those used during China's Cultural Revolution. Hain condemned the farm occupations, and described the attacks at the march as "thuggery orchestrated from on high."[4]

Zimbabwe's government viewed the removal of funds for land reform by the British government as a breach of the Lancaster House Agreement and an infringement of national sovereignty. In light of this, the constitutional committee's proposals were implemented on April 6 and the Constitution was amended to transfer the obligation to pay for land resettlement from Zimbabwe to Britain. In the future, the government of Zimbabwe would only pay for improvements such as irrigation, dams, farm buildings and so on. As the number of occupied farms rose to 975, Mugabe gave his unqualified support to the squatters: "Those who have invaded the farms, they are going to stay. I support them. We will not remove them."

The murder of 25-year-old Police Constable Finashe Chikwenya on April 4 by ZANU-PF was further proof, if any more was needed, that Mugabe's supporters considered themselves to be above the law. The policeman had arrested three squatters who had attacked a white farmer and almost beaten him to death; for arresting them, Chikwenga paid the ultimate price. Needless to say, the suspects were released without being charged for their violent act.

Prominent among the leaders of the ZANU-PF mobs was Chakwana Mueri, otherwise known as "Comrade Jesus," who incited mobs of drugged and drunken supporters to rampage through white farms in an orgy of looting, burning, beating and destruction; the goal of this was to force the white farmers to sign away the rights to their farms on the spot.

As the war veterans, with Mugabe's connivance, drove white farmers from their properties and burned the homes of the farmers' black employees who became homeless and penniless vagrants, rendering the hitherto prosperous farms barren and unproductive, Mugabe turned his attention to the courts. Curiously enough, throughout these troubled times, a British military team was present in Zimbabwe at Mugabe's invitation in order to help train his forces.

At that point, even some cabinet members were beginning to doubt the wisdom of allowing the farm invasions to continue, and they made this clear at a meeting convened when Mugabe was visiting Cuba. At a press conference held on April 13, Vice-President Msika declared that, in view of the amendments to the Constitution that allowed white farms to be seized without compensation, "it [was] no longer necessary to continue with these demonstrations." On the same day, Judge Moses Chinhengo stated that the farm invasions must be brought to an end. Once again, Mugabe ignored the court, and the number of farm invasions rose to 1,100.

On April 15, a car containing three MDC supporters was bombed by ZANU-PF. Talent Mabika, a 23-year-old MDC official, and Tichaona Chiminya, Morgan Tsvangirai's 38-year-old personal driver, were burned to death. On the same day, 47-year-old white farmer and MDC supporter David Stevens and his foreman Julius Andoche were abducted from their Arizona Farm and taken to the local office of the War Veterans' Association. From there they were driven to the local ZANU-PF headquarters, taken into the bush, and beaten and shot to death. A neighboring farmer, John Osborne, who went to Stevens' aid, was also severely beaten. Stevens' farm laborers resisted the squatters and seriously injured one of them in the process. As revenge, Arizona Farm, along with its vast tobacco sheds and the homes of its 300 black farmworkers, was razed to the ground. As Mugabe's airplane returned to Harare from Cuba, two other white farmers lay bound in a cave, having been tortured for hours on end and beaten senseless. Mugabe, however, was unrepentant. He said that the fighting was "a struggle that cannot be corrected by the courts."

Suddenly, a ray of hope appeared. On April 17, 2000, Tim Henwood, president of the Commercial Farmers' Union (CFU) met with Mugabe at State House for about an hour and a half. Mugabe was conciliatory, spoke of land reform without violence, and promised to restore law and order soon. This glimmer of hope was quickly extinguished. Within 18 hours, white farmer Martin Olds was shot and hacked to death at Compensation Farm in Matabeleland, after he tried to defend himself with his shotgun and pistol against the AK-47 assault rifles of his ZANU-PF attackers. Officers from the nearby Nyamandlovu Police Station prevented neighboring whites from coming to his rescue, and his attackers were allowed to get away. Following this atrocity, the CFU ordered that all white farms in Matabeleland be evacuated, whereupon all but a handful of their occupants loaded what provisions they could into cars and trucks and drove to the relative safety of Bulawayo.

The white exodus from the land now extended from Matabeleland to include Midlands, Virginia, Karoi, Enterprise, Chinhoyi, Hwedza and Macheke—the core of the country's agricultural heartland. Now began a white stampede by all those with British citizenship to leave the country; large queues formed outside the British High Commission in Harare.

The terrorism continued relentlessly. Supporters and security guards, even those in the act of addressing rallies, were beaten, raped and murdered by those who knew they were exempt from the law; and names and addresses of MDC activists were obtained by torturing men, women and children. The courage of MDC members shone through like a beacon in a dark world, but as the months and years went by, the number willing to risk their lives, and those of their friends and families, by attending Tsvangirai's rallies dwindled from the thousands to just a few dozen.

By then, ZANU-PF's campaign of intimidation had spread into Harare, where Hunzvi's "surgery" office (he claimed he had qualified as a doctor while in Poland in the 1970s) served as headquarters for his ZANU-PF torturers. On May 7, the same day that white farmer Alan Dunn's skull was fractured when he was attacked by a gang of six men, Hunzvi declared that the ZANU-PF were "going to search for these people with British passports to leave our country." Meanwhile, opposition leader Tsvangirai vented his frustration. "There is violence everywhere, absolutely everywhere," he said. "We have no access to the media, we cannot campaign, we are being harassed all the time. How can there be free and fair elections?"

Mugabe began ZANU-PF's campaign for the election of June 24–25. The Party message was unchanged. "The end has come. Land will now come to the people." As for the MDC, "They started the violence. Now they are getting more than they bargained for." On May 15, by which time 1,400 farms had been invaded, the Zimbabwe Human Rights Forum recorded that there had been 19 deaths, 1,012 assaults and 8 rapes since the referendum, and that 86 percent of the recorded violations had been perpetrated by ZANU-PF. These figures were clearly a gross understatement, in a country where reporting any abuse, however trivial, meant risking one's life. Despite this, Don McKinnon, secretary-general of the Commonwealth, which had provided a team of 40 observers, still believed it possible for there to be free elections."

How did South Africa, the country that supplied Zimbabwe with 55 percent of its electricity and one-third of its fuel, react to the events on its northern border? Archbishop Desmond Tutu condemned Mugabe in strident terms. "He's almost a caricature of all the things people think black leaders do," he said. "He seems to be wanting to make a cartoon of himself." Nelson Mandela expressed his shock at Mugabe's "use of violence and the corroding of the rule of law." Of immediate concern to South Africa's president, Thabo Mbeki, was the damage to the South African economy caused by having to cope with tens of thousands of economic migrants who were pouring across the border from Zimbabwe, when unemployment in South Africa was already at 30 percent.

Mbeki spoke to Mugabe during a summit of African leaders held at the Victoria Falls on April 21, 2000. When the two met again in Bulawayo on May 5, Mbeki, who in his own country had to contend with a sizable black lobby who favored forcibly seizing land from whites, obtained assurances from Mugabe that law and order would be restored. However, as usual, nothing changed.

With much of Zimbabwe, especially the rural areas, held in the grip of terror, MDC leader Tsvangirai was virtually confined to Harare. His rallies were held amidst tight security, as those who attended them would be hunted down by ZANU-PF mobs. Anyone who did not have a ZANU-PF T-shirt or a ZANU-PF party card was in grave danger.

In the June 2 issue of *The Herald*, 804 more farms were identified (gazetted) for "compulsory acquisition" and, rather than become embroiled in the bureaucracy of the 1992 Land Acquisition Act, a "Fast Track" resettlement program was to begin. To anyone bold enough to criticize his decision, Mugabe's reply was, "Where was the rule of law when our land was seized by the Rhodesians?" On July 2, a further 2,237 farms were gazetted, bringing the number of seized farms to 3,041.

When Mugabe held ZANU-PF's final rally on Zimbabwe Grounds in Harare's Highfield township, a mere 3,000 people gathered there, as compared with the hundreds of thousands who had turned out to greet him on his return from exile in 1980. By contrast, over 25,000 people attended Tsvangirai's final rally, held in the Rufaro Stadium in Harare's Mbare township. As the polling booths opened, the Zimbabwe Human Rights Forum reported 37 murders, 2,466 assaults, 27 rapes and 617 abductions during the election campaign; 10,000 people had been displaced, and 90.7 percent of these offenses had been perpetrated by ZANU-PF.

The final result announced on June 27, 2000, was that ZANU-PF earned 62 Seats; the MDC, 57 seats; and the independents, 1 seat. However, when all the votes were counted, it was found that 79,827 more people had voted against Mugabe than for him. Mugabe, who awarded ZANU-PF 30 seats before the election had begun, therefore emerged with control of 92 of the 150 parliamentary seats.

Tony Yengeni, chief whip in the South African Parliament and leader of that country's observer team in Zimbabwe, concluded that "the results of the parliamentary elections broadly reflect the will of the Zimbabwean people." However, Pierre Schori, a former Swedish cabinet minister who headed the European Union's observer group of 190, referred to the "high levels of violence, intimidation and coercion" that "marred the election campaign." Schori felt that the words "free and fair" did not apply to these elections. Jonathan Moyo's reaction was predictable, and the European Union was added to the list of "forces trying to overthrow the Mugabe government." Don McKinnon reported that "the violence which disfigured this campaign was employed systematically as part of a strategy to diminish support for the opposition parties."

Mugabe saw the the MDC as an attempt by Tsvangirai, the white Rhodesians, the British and South African governments, and Nkomo's ZAPU to undermine him. There was a grain of truth in this. After all, none of them had any reason to rejoice over the prospect of Zimbabwe becoming a one-party state under a Marxist dictator.

However, as usual, Mugabe reacted to this view with disproportionate heavy-handedness. He colluded with the war veterans (many of whom were not even war veterans technically) by paying them an allowance to occupy white farms, and when the whites were driven out he showed no concern whatsoever, either for their welfare or for their black employees. When the court demanded that the squatters leave the land, Mugabe simply refused to recognize its jurisdiction. To Mugabe, anyone who was white was labeled "British," whatever their country of origin. It was now a case of "British, get out!" and he sought to remove whites from their positions in all state and private concerns.

In the 2000 elections, Mugabe showed that he was prepared to go to any lengths to obliterate the opposition. He tampered with the electoral process in order to give himself an extra 30 unearned parliamentary seats; he prevented the international monitors from doing their work; and he sent mobs to intimidate MDC supporters.

Meanwhile, more and more white farms were commandeered without compensation or put out of business by the actions of the war veteran squatters. Mugabe threw all foreign journalists out of Zimbabwe in an unsuccessful attempt to hide what was going on from the outside world.

10

Mugabe Tightens His Grip

On October 16, 2000, riots broke out in the townships of Harare following a 34 percent increase in the price of bread. Instead of addressing the problem, the government saw it as an opportunity to attack the MDC, which was particularly strong in that area. First, military helicopters bombed the crowds with canisters of tear gas, then trained soldiers of the Parachute Regiment, armed with clubs and whips beat everyone they could lay their hands on: their violence extended even to the very young.

Tabo Mbeki, worried that events in Zimbabwe would destabilize South Africa and frighten away foreign investors, visited Mugabe on August 2. He received the same assurances about law and order being restored and war veterans being removed from white farms; again, nothing changed.

With the occupation of more farms, CFU decided to take action. The legality of the Fast Track resettlement program would be challenged in the courts, and the CFU would lend its support to a general strike. Its president, Tim Henwood, said that "it may soon be impossible for farming operations to continue nationwide." However, the strike received a mixed reception. The Zimbabwe Congress of Trade Unions and the MDC were supportive of it, but the Conference of Zimbabwe Industries was against it. Seeing the weakness of his position, Henwood withdrew his legal challenge in favor of seeking "meaningful dialogue" with the government, but the anger of his union's farmers was so great, he was forced to reinstate the legal appeal.

Tsvangirai, at the Rufaro Stadium rally, referred to Mugabe, saying, "If you don't want to go peacefully, we will remove you violently." This gave the authorities the perfect excuse to announce that Tsvangirai would be charged with "incitement to violence."

On October 25, the 57 MPs of the MDC demanded Mugabe's impeachment and removal from office for "gross misconduct" and "willful violation of the Constitution." This was unrealistic, because impeachment required a two-thirds majority vote. In any event, because of the inactivity of the Speaker, Emmerson Mnangagwa, a loyal supporter of Mugabe, the motion was never put before the House.

The CFU's appeal to the Supreme Court to have the Fast Track seizures of land declared illegal was heard by Manchester-born and Cambridge-educated Anthony Gubbay, a 68-year-old chief justice who found in the CFU's favour. Mugabe, in blatant defiance, immediately appeared on television and declared that "whatever the courts might say on the matter, the land is ours and we will take it." More white farms were invaded and more white farmers were murdered (six murders took place between April and December 2000). Meanwhile, "Comrade Jesus" was rewarded with a 1,000-acre tobacco farm, and Mugabe declared amnesty for all those who had committed political violence between January and July. According to figures released by Tobacco Sales Floor Ltd., tobacco sales between 1990 and 2000 had fallen by a massive 80 percent.

Political spokesman Jonathan Moyo, who was head of propaganda, demanded that Joe Winter, a BBC reporter, leave the country within 24 hours, and a mob was sent to Winter's house to reinforce the message. Also in the firing line was 68-year-old Chief Justice Gubbay, who had ruled against the Fast Track land reforms. On December 22, Hunzvi issued an ultimatum to the Supreme Court's judges, giving them 14 days to resign.

The *Daily News*, Zimbabwe's only independent newspaper, had long been a thorn in Mugabe's side, and it was becoming increasingly outspoken. "Impeach Mugabe!" was a front-page headline, and the *News* accused ZANU-PF of "betraying our true heroes." The paper also rejoiced in the fact that President Kabila of the Congo, one of Mugabe's few remaining allies on behalf of whom 11,000 Zimbabwean troops were currently engaged, had been assassinated. Retribution for the newspaper came in the early hours of January 28, 2001, when its printing press was destroyed in a shattering explosion, believed to have been caused by several anti-tank mines attached to a detonator. However, the *Daily News* obtained another printing press and did not miss printing a single issue from that point forward, until it was finally shut down in September 2003.

On March 2, 2001, Chief Justice Gubbay agreed to take leave until his official retirement on July 1; this was prompted by his court having been invaded by a mob who prevented him from entering it. Now, led by Hunzvi, attacks began on Harare's white-owned businesses including shops and hotels, even hospitals and aid organizations. However, the raiding of 18 South African companies was a step too far and Zimbabwe's high commissioner in Pretoria was summoned for a severe reprimand. On June 4, Hunzvi died in Bulawayo of an AIDS-related condition and was declared a "national hero."

Daily Telegraph reporter David Blair was expelled from Zimbabwe on June 30 after Jonathan Moyo refused to renew Blair's work permit. Five weeks later, 50 more farms were looted, bringing the total number of farms under squatter-occupation to over 900. When white farmers came to the aid of one of their colleagues, 21 of them were imprisoned and humiliated. On June 29, *The Herald* published the names of another 2,030 white farms that were to be seized. The maize crop yield had fallen by 42 percent in 2001, and a report by the Famine Early Warning Network indicated that the country would face famine in early 2002.

On September 7, at a Commonwealth foreign ministers' meeting in Nigeria's capital, Abuja, Britain offered the sum of £36 million for land reform, as long as the redistribution was done legally and peacefully and was combined with macroeconomic reforms.[1] Mugabe, however, continued with his preexisting agenda. The Land Acquisition Act was amended, whereby any farmer served with a "Section 8 Occupation Order" had three months to vacate his farm, and this would apply retroactively. Having appointed his own chief justice, and expanded the Supreme Court's judiciary from five to eight judges, (with the extra three judges being linked to ZANU-PF), Mugabe could now be sure of the court's support.

It was then time to remove the final vestiges of electoral opposition. In future elections, anyone wishing to register to vote had to produce title deeds or rental agreements of utility bills as proof of residence. This meant that hundreds of thousands of urban MDC supporters living in shacks in the townships would be disenfranchised. In the rural areas, anyone wishing to vote must first obtain the personal approval of the village headmen, all of whom were in the pay of the government. The murder of a war veteran on November 5 in Bulawayo gave Mugabe the excuse to burn down the MDC's regional headquarters.

On November 30, Mugabe's "Media and Information Commission" was empowered to prevent journalists from working and to close down newspapers. Inflation was 97.9 percent, unemployment was at 60 percent; on December 14 the United Nations World Food Program announced that 558,000 Zimbabweans needed food aid immediately. Since the referendum, there had been 81 political killings and 39 more black farmworkers had been murdered by squatters.

Strangely enough, all whites, no matter what their country of origin, were referred to by the Mugabe regime as "British," despite the fact that people from many lands dwelt in Zimbabwe—Italians in particular were especially numerous. On January 6, 2002, anyone with dual nationality was told that they must either accept only Zimbabwean nationality or they must leave the country. Those who chose to leave found that airfares were prohibitively expensive. In 1990, it cost more than Z$300,000 to fly to Britain, whereas only 18 months before it cost Z$38,000. An added difficulty was that foreign currency could no longer be purchased easily when Z$3.60 were worth £1, and now Z$79 were required to buy £1.

In February 2002, sanctions were imposed to prevent Mugabe and his officials from traveling to Europe and America. On March 9 and 10, presidential elections were held for Zimbabwe's 5.6 million voters; four days later, it was announced that 78-year-old Robert Mugabe had won, earning 56 percent of the votes compared with his rival Morgan Tsvangirai's MDU party's 40 percent.

On March 15, two days after he returned to power once more,

Mugabe introduced the Access to Information and Protection of Privacy Act. The effect of this was to prevent journalists from working in Zimbabwe without the approval of a government commission headed by Jonathan Moyo.[2]

The same day, the Commonwealth Observer Group, present in Zimbabwe to ensure a free and fair election, reported that "a high level of politically motivated violence and intimidation" was present on both sides, but most violence was principally committed by ZANU-PF and specifically by its paramilitary youth wing, which led the group to conclude that "the conditions in Zimbabwe did not adequately allow for a free expression of will by the electors." Sickening pictures of MDU supporters being viciously beaten appeared on televisions throughout the world. Hideous injuries were inflicted on those who failed to support ZANU-PF; hundreds of MDU polling agents were abducted or intimidated; and the identity cards of MDU supporters were stolen in order to disenfranchise them. Subsequently, on March 19, Zimbabwe was suspended from the councils of the Commonwealth for one year.

In the words of Welshman Ncube, secretary-general of the MDC, "Many of our election agents are missing, and hundreds of people have fled from all over Mashonaland West Province. It is absolutely appalling. It appears there is a systematic hunting-down of people who voted for or helped the MDC during the elections."[3] Some voters were simply prohibited from voting, including former prime minister Sir Garfield Todd, then 93.[4]

Mugabe's victory in the elections emboldened Erasmus Marufu, his brother-in-law, to install himself surreptitiously as secretary to a small but profitable British-owned herb and spice exporting business, known as Four Seasons. Marufu used the pretext of a minor labor dispute to lock out Chris Dunbar, its managing director, who had previously been a recipient of death threats.[5]

On Monday March 18, 2002, Terry Ford, a white farmer from Norton, which was 25 miles west of Harare, was attacked with axes by Mugabe's so-called war veterans and he was then run over and shot in the head. Pictures of his body, covered in a blanket with his faithful dog sitting next to him, were shown all around the world. Ford's crime was to refuse to hand over his farm. Was it a coincidence that

Mugabe's sister, Sabina, had visited Ford 16 months earlier and informed him that she required his farmstead so she could move in? Sabina had been MP for Zvimba, Mugabe's home district, since 1985 and was finance secretary for the ZANU-PF women's league. Ford was not the first white farmer she had visited in her black Mercedes-Benz. Her son, Innocent, had been director of the government's repressive Central Intelligence Organisation (the secret police)[6] until his death in 2001, and her second son, Leo, owned a construction consortium, which obtained lucrative contracts for the construction of public buildings.[7] Ford was the tenth white farmer to be murdered in the previous two years.

According to the English newspaper the *Daily Telegraph*, inflation in Zimbabwe had almost reached 120 percent, six out of ten people were jobless, and the gross domestic product per head had fallen in 2001 to £270 (from £290 in 2000). Visitors to Zimbabwe found permanent riot police guards in every supermarket to prevent looting. The price of a box of tissues was the equivalent of £10.50p sterling; a tube of toothpaste, £9; a jar of women's foundation cream, £55, and a roll of toilet paper, £2.50, if you could find it! There was no ground-maize, the staple diet, or sugar for sale whatsoever.

Gasoline, however, supplied by Libya, was still available. (Zimbabwe's government had in exchange issued 10,000 passports to Libyan citizens.) There were also many Afghans to be seen in Harare's market place.

President Thabo Mbeki of South Africa, in a signed statement that appeared on the ANC website, referred to the election thus: "While the process was clearly not perfect, the ANC believes that the people of Zimbabwe have spoken."[8] Mbeki's failure to condemn Mugabe led to a loss of confidence in his country by the outside world, and the South African rand lost 32 percent of its value between March 2001 and March 2002.[9] Nevertheless, South Africa, which supplied Zimbabwe with its electricity and vital food supplies, was in a unique position to apply pressure on Mugabe. However, cutting off supplies of these precious commodities would undoubtedly trigger an enormous increase in the number of refugees flooding across the Zimbabwe borders.[10]

Tsvangirai revealed that he had been charged with attempting to assassinate Mugabe, on the basis of a videotape in which he referred to Mugabe as needing to be "eliminated." However, in his defense, Tsvangirai maintained claims that he was framed, and that the "elimination" he spoke of was meant via the ballot box only and had no sinister meaning.[11]

In June 2002, Mugabe defied the will of the international community by attending—with his wife Grace and an entourage of nearly 20—a U.N. World Food Summit in Rome, where he was urged by Secretary General Kofi Annan to relax governmental controls on grain and permit a free market.[12] Mugabe refused. "The West," he said, "enjoys seeing people suffer."[13] Mugabe of course was blind to the suffering of his own people because of his destructive policies. One example of such abandonment of Zimbabweans is in the story of Venenzia Tanyanyiwa. In late May 2002, Venenzia, a 24-year-old mother of three, returned from her work as a prostitute, doused herself in paraffin, and set herself on fire. The reason she gave for doing this was simply that she and her children were hungry. "My children are always crying for food," she said. "I could not provide, and I was so stressed that I thought the only way out was to kill myself." Her husband had abandoned her and the children and they were receiving no maintenance. Because she could not prove her identity, she was not entitled to social welfare. Furthermore, her water supply had been cut off due to an unpaid bill. Six months later, Venenzia still suffered pain, despite treatment, and the only meal she received each day was supper, but, since October 2002, the Highfield Church of Nazareth provided two meals per day for her children.[14]

11

Disaster Looms

The widespread seizure of white-owned farms continued unabated. One account of such a seizure was printed in *The Mail on Sunday*, written by Jane Laing, an eyewitness. In June 2002, Laing, a British citizen, traveled to Zimbabwe with her three children and her partner, Sebastian Rous. They were en route to Rous' farm at Karandera, north of Harare.

There, to Jane's horror, they were surrounded for four days by about 200 blacks, many of whom were Sebastian's former loyal employees. Describing themselves as "trade unionists," the blacks patrolled the perimeter fence with "machetes at their sides 24 hours a day." When Adam, a loyal black farm manager, tried to intervene, he was marched "six miles to the police station by a vicious gang of thugs."

Laing described "ominous and threatening" chanting, where the men were "baying" for their blood, and she also wrote of the ferocious drum-beating of their captors, who demanded Z$7.6 million (equivalent to £86,000), which they did not possess. Laing, her children, and Rous had no choice but to abandon the farm, which for the past 20 years had produced "rich harvests of tobacco, maize, soya beans and passion fruit," and return to Britain.[1]

Many other farmers were also faced with not having a choice. At midnight on June 23, 2002, the Final Notices of Acquisition, which gave 2,900 of Zimbabwe's remaining 3,500 white farmers notice to cease their operations immediately, and vacate their farms by mid–August, came into effect. Those who refused to leave would face up to two years' imprisonment. The government was unwilling to extend the deadline to enable the farmers to finish grading their tobacco crop—which once provided the country with 30 percent of its foreign currency. Twenty-three-year-old farmer Marcus Hale, of Nyabira north of Harare, summed up the farmers' frustration: "We tried to do a deal with the war veterans…. We planted about 150 acres of wheat for them because they don't know how to farm. We were supposed to share the profits, but they forced us off."[2] In that same week, Harare's shops ran out of bread and the British *Daily Telegraph* newspaper published an advertisement asking people to contribute funds to alleviate Zimbabwe's famine. If only Mugabe had learned from the example of Malawi's President Banda, who was enlightened enough to encourage white civil servants and businessmen to remain at their posts in his newly independent country, until his own countrymen were ready to take over the reins of power.

"Everyone's given up on [the courts]," said Jim Sinclair, who had been driven off his farm at Norton, 50 miles from Harare. He stressed the difficulties facing the two million blacks who were living on white farms. "They have nowhere else to go; and once those farms close they have no jobs and no food. Nobody in government seems to care. They show a complete lack of concern about the famine."[3] Ian Smith remained defiant, saying, "I'm going down to my farm this weekend, and we'll be producing food flat out!"[4]

In June 2002, Sydney Masamvu, writing in *The Financial Gazette*, compared life in Zimbabwe with life in Mozambique. He pointed out that both countries helped each other as they fought their bitter wars of liberation in the 1970s. When Samora Machel came to power in Mozambique in 1986, he faced an uphill struggle, after years of civil war and poverty. However, he was successful and Mozambique's economy was booming, the country was politically stable, and democracy was entrenched. The same could not be said of Zimbabwe, where Mugabe was "increasingly emerging as the odd man out in the present crop of leaders in Southern Africa."[5]

Mugabe convened a meeting in July 2002 of his military chiefs to discuss the acquisition of a squadron of MiG-29SE fighter jets—

the official cost was £20 million per aircraft. These jets were said to be urgently required, but it was not clear why they were needed. At this meeting, Air Vice-Marshall R. Mhlanga suggested that the person to underwrite this purchase might be Nicholas van Hoogstraten.

The 57-year-old van Hoogstraten was recently found guilty by an Old Bailey jury of the manslaughter of a business associate. (On December 8, 2003, van Hoogstraten's conviction for manslaughter was overturned by the Court of Appeal, on the grounds that the "case against him did not stand up legally."[6]) He had connections with Zimbabwe going back to the mid–1980's. It was then that he purchased an 8 percent stake in Willoughby's (part of the Lonrho empire) with interests in mining and land. Since then, van Hoogstraten's stake had risen to 70 percent, and included the vast Zimbabwean estates of Central, Eastdale and Essexdale.

In return for his services, van Hoogstraten would be granted another 1.2 million acres of land, but how he would conduct the operation from within Belmont prison in South London was not explained.

In Zimbabwe, van Hoogstraten had a private army of 150 armed men, and a luxury villa in the Italian style: admittedly not as grandiose as his partially built Sussex mansion with its estimated cost of £40 million. Such was his influence, that when squatters invaded his land he was able to persuade the local governor of the Midlands Province to keep them under control. (12/6)

In July 2002, Andrew Meldrum, the *Economist*'s (and the *Guardian*'s) correspondent in Zimbabwe, was acquitted by magistrate Godfrey Machey of "publishing a falsehood." However, Mugabe was so desperate to rid himself of all foreign correspondents that Meldrum was served with a deportation order as he left the court. Meldrum appealed and won leave to take his case to the Supreme Court—a process that could take several months.[8]

At Parliament's annual opening in July 2002, Mugabe hailed the land redistribution scheme as "an unparalleled success" and announced that almost half of the 5,000 white-owned commercial farms had been transferred to blacks. Currency was trading then at Z$1,000 to every £1.[9]

Mugabe also traveled to Cuba, hoping to enlist the support of one of his few remaining friends, President Fidel Castro. Mugabe could not afford to keep up the payments on a Z$360 million loan provided by Libya's Colonel Qaddafi, to whom he had already mortgaged a sizable portion of Zimbabwe's farms, hotels and oil installations. It was unlikely, however, that Cuba, itself an impoverished country, would be able to help him.

A letter from five members of the House of Lords (published in *The Daily Telegraph* on July 31, 2002) stated that food aid was reported to be going to Zimbabwe but distributed on a political basis; only those who could produce a ZANU-PF party card would obtain aid. The letter urged that observers be put in place as soon as possible to ensure that starving people received the food aid that was intended for them, no matter what political views they had.

On July 26, 2002, Joshua Malinga, Zimbabwe's deputy secretary for disability and a member of the Politburo, was traveling to New York to attend a conference on disability when he was arrested and detained at Gatwick Airport. This was under the terms of the E.U. ban, which included Mugabe and 72 of his associates and members of the ruling party and their families. Malinga returned home the following day.[9] In a tit-for-tat retaliation for Britain's expulsion of Joshua Malinga, four British nationals traveling to Zimbabwe were denied entry.[10]

On August 12, 2002 Mugabe addressed a crowd of people at National Heroes Acre, Harare, the burial place of those who, in the eyes of himself and his ruling ZANU-PF party, have done well for their country.[11]

The first part of his speech was taken up by his eulogy for the recently departed Dr. Bernard Chidzero, whom he described as an "intellectual, soft-spoken, industrious, imaginative and adventitious writer, planner, administrator, internationalist, minister and politician, and loving father." (Chidzero had been economic minister of development and the finance minister in Mugabe's government.)

Mugabe was due to confer upon Chidzero the Order of the Zimbabwe Star, an award given to "men and women of stature" who had made "remarkable contributions to the stability, development, and prosperity of Zimbabwe and humanity in general." This honor would now have to be conferred posthumously on another occasion. Dr. Chidzero, said Mugabe, had been part of the "revolutionary Tradition" of a people struggling against "the political and economic calculations and dictates of oppressor nations of the west—now the European Union and America." Mugabe said that these "imperialist forces" wished to control and manipulate Zimbabweans' lives and destiny and exploit their wealth and resources.

Those who were buried in Heroes Acre died for the return of their lands, which had been held by sons of "colonial oppressors." "Colonialism came from the European Union," said Mugabe. The Europeans were the same people "who massacred us only yesterday to prevent the onset of the same democracy they claim to want to usher in today." Mugabe then attacked democracy in general. The "so-called free world" had enslaved, colonized, discriminated, massacred, plundered, and expropriated. Ironically, Mugabe could have been describing his own administration.

Mugabe then went on to praise the "new war veterans"—those young men and women who "slugged it out on the farms in support of their elder veterans." The young people of the country had a mandatory duty to "love and defend" Zimbabwe, and they could demonstrate their commitment by joining the National Youth Service Program. However, according to Morgan Tsvangirai, this meant that sons and daughters would be "forcibly drafted ... and be transformed into killing machines for the perpetuation of Mugabe's dictatorship." Not only would the children be turned into killers, but they would, particularly the girls, be subjected to sexual slavery by their "uncouth trainers." Tsvangarai stated that he would never allow children to be turned into troops for Mugabe's evil regime.

The end of August was to be the deadline by which farm resettlement would be complete. Mugabe wished that "everyone interested in farming should be on the land by the time the rains come."

No speech by Mugabe would be complete without an attack on Britain, of course. "To those who want to earn this country for Britain, and govern it for the British Empire as in the past, we say here on this national shrine that the game is up and it is time for them to go. There is no place for rapacious supremecists here." Again Mugabe's rhetoric ignores the fact that the British Empire ceased to exist many decades ago, Britain in the end being only too pleased to make former colonies—including those in Africa—independent. Today, Britain has virtually no influence in Zimbabwe, as dispossessed white farmers whose ancestors came from Britain, but who have no British passports, know only too well.

As far as feeding the nation was concerned, Mugabe allowed that Zimbabwe would continue to import grain until the following season. "We remain determined to ensure that no Zimbabwean starves to death," said Mugabe.

Tsvangirai had many criticisms of Mugabe's speech. He saw Dr. Chidzero as an internationalist, an illustrious and cosmopolitan son of Zimbabwe, who abhorred racialism, tribalism and all divisive practices. Tsvangirai saw that Mugabe had used the occasion of Chidzero's death to "disgorge a message of violence and hate" that was "the very antithesis of what the life of Dr. Chidzero signified."[12]

Tsvangarai also saw the matter of Zimbabwe's recovery in a totally different light. The country was reeling from the effects of Mugabe's dictatorship, with millions facing certain death from disease, starvation and state-sponsored violence. In fact, everything was in short supply in Zimbabwe except misery, starvation and death. Mugabe's regime had reduced innocent citizens to the actions of scavenging animals.

On August 15, 2002, Foreign Office Minister Peter Hain said that Zimbabwe's was "the world's fastest shrinking economy, declining at a rate of 10 percent last year and another 11 percent this year." Two days later, 20 more white farmers across Zimbabwe had been rounded up and imprisoned in police cells for failing to obey Mugabe's eviction order. Six of the farmers, including a provisional leader of the CFU, subsequently appeared before magistrates and were released on Z$5,000 bail (about £5), and were charged on September 6 with having failed to vacate their farms by the agreed-upon deadline.[13]

On August 22, 2002, British opposition leader Ian Duncan Smith urged Prime Minister Tony Blair to boycott a speech that Mugabe was to make at the forthcoming ten-day U.N. World Summit for Sustainable Development in Johannesburg, beginning on August 26. Shadow Foreign Secretary Michael Ancrum went further and urged Blair to refuse to participate in any matters brought up at the summit that related to African development. It was the Conservative Party's view that neither Zimbabwe's neighbors in the Southern Africa development community nor Mr. Mbeki's New Partnership for Africa had taken a firm enough stand on the subject of Mugabe's excesses.[14]

A vociferous, placard-carrying contingent of MDC supporters from Zimbabwe were present at the summit, demanding the ousting of Mugabe from power. Also present was the South African Landless Peoples' Movement, which held the opposite view. Mangaliso Kubheka, its leader, said that his movement "support[ed] the giving of land to landless people and [supported] Mr. Mugabe." His followers had already clashed with the South African police and 73 of them had been arrested.[15]

Despite Mugabe's anti–British, anti–American and anti–European rhetoric, aid from foreign countries continued to pour in, and Mugabe, despite his avowed principles, did not see fit to return a single penny of it. In 2002, the European Community (EC) allocated £83 million for food aid to Zimbabwe, and another £5 million for "ongoing development projects in direct support of the population in the social sectors," and in the fields of "democratisation, respect for human rights and the rule of law." The United States, in the year ending September 30, 2002, provided $17.2 million for the treatment and prevention of disease caused by HIV and for microfinancial economic programs.[16] Mugabe's response to this generosity was to say, "What do I need Europe for?" In the future, he would promote stronger ties with Asian States, such as Malaysia.

Despite Mugabe's attempts to break their spirits, some white farmers have found ways to prosper. Thomas Niehaus, having been deprived of his farm at Chetugu, 65 miles southwest of Harare, discovered a new way to make a living for himself, his wife and their two children: many other former farmers are doing the same. Niehaus staked a claim on a 24-acre site that was part of his former farm, and on it he established a mill with cyanide tanks and carbon filters. Villagers now bring their soil and ores to the mill, which they rent from him, and they in turn make a living by selling what the mill produces: nuggets of 65–85 percent pure gold. Niehaus is the only remaining farmer (out of 17 in his area) who is still able to make a living from the land.

Today, another surviving farming couple, Nigel and Clare Hough, have an ostrich farm (and they produce ostrich-skin bags and shoes for export) at Marondera, once Zimbabwe's largest tobacco-growing area. They are the only whites to remain; their 23 neighboring farmers gave up the unequal struggle and abandoned their farms.

The Houghs also keep cattle, one of which is stolen every week by squatters, who leave only a skeleton for the Houghs to find the following day—all the meat having been removed. Generators and electric cables have also been stolen. There is also an orphanage on the farm, which the Houghs built for the children of deceased farm laborers; one in three of these children die from AIDS.[17]

Are the black people who have been resettled on previously white-owned farms happy with their lot? One of them, Lydia Muzenda, 62, certainly is not. Seeds, fertilizers and tractors promised by the government failed to materialize. Without the means to plow and sow, she can only watch as the rains wash away the topsoil, rendering the land progressively less fertile. With hundreds of thousands of others like her, she is destitute.[18] Mugabe has not grasped the point that making one section of the population poorer does not necessarily make the rest (i.e., the majority) richer.

12

The Earth Summit
and Beyond

On September 2, 2002, Mugabe addressed the Earth Summit in Johannesburg, where he accused the "willful few in the north [northern Hemisphere]" of reducing the rest of mankind to "collective underdogs," and "chattels of the rich" and who "beat, batter and bully ... under the dirty cover of democracy." There were the usual references to "imperial interests" and "hegemonic ambitions." "The rule of law, democracy and governance are values that we cherish because we fought for them against the very same people who today ... preach to us." It was the inequitable access to land that caused poverty, starvation and a lack of development in Zimbabwe. Mugabe believed that the "right holders" to this land were the black majority. However, he did not intend to deprive the white farmers of land completely. Every one of them would be entitled to at least one farm.[1]

Economically, Zimbabwe (22 years after Independence), was still an "occupied country." Therefore, his government had decided to do "the only right and just thing"—taking the land back and "giving it to its rightful, indigenous, black owners, who lost it in circumstances of colonial pillage."

At the Earth Summit, Tony Blair said that "the government of Zimbabwe ... is a gross and appalling catalogue of incompetence, mismanagement and corruption."[2] However, Blair and his colleagues were surprised at the level of support for Mugabe among some of the other southern African countries. President Joaquim Chissano of Mozambique said Mugabe's land reform policy was aimed at achieving "a balanced distribution of land among all Zimbabwean people."[3] Namibia's President Sam Nujoma went even further and ordered as a first step the expropriation of 192 farms belonging to "non-resident foreigners." He accused Britain of enslaving, colonizing and robbing his country.[4]

Mugabe, by his actions, had demonstrated that, in his uncompromising view, white commercial farmers must not only vacate their farms, but they must also leave the country, as they were not "proper" Zimbabweans. However, in *The Daily News* on September 19, 2002, Saul Gwakuba Ndlovu takes issue with Mugabe. "How can an unborn baby decide its place or country of birth?" he asks; although many colonial regimes evicted people from their homes in times gone by, "could one wrong action correct another wrong action?" Ndlovu points out the illogicality of Mugabe's actions, citing the example of Dr. Bernard Chidzero who, when he died, received the great honor of being buried at Heroes Acre, despite the fact that, although he was Zimbabwe-born, Chidzero was of Malawian descent. Ndlovu also wonders whether the same eviction instructions would be given to other groups whose ethnic ancestors were not Zimbabwean?[5]

On September 23, 2002, the troika of President Thabo Mbeki of South Africa, President Olusegun Obasanjo of Nigeria, and Prime Minister John Howard of Australia, failed to reach agreement over the toughening of Commonwealth sanctions against Zimbabwe concerning its controversial land reform and political policies.[6]

In that same month, the government of Zimbabwe, not content with confiscating farms from their rightful owners, gazetted legislation ordering that these dispossessed farmers pay "retrenchment" money to their former employees. Apparently no upper limit had been set as to the amount an employee may seek, even if he or she had worked on a farm for as little as one month. For example, someone earning Z$10,000 per month could seek a retrenchment package of Z$500,000 or even Z$750,000. Half the money must be paid out by the farmer when he vacates the farm, and the balance must be paid when, if ever, the farmer receives compensation from the government. In the event that the farmer does not have the money to pay, an angry mob would arrive at his home and demand that he sell his possessions in order to meet the bill. The results are predictable: the new owner is invariably one of Mugabe's henchmen, and soon the fields are denuded of both crops and cattle.[7] If a new recipient is unused to managing what to him is an enormous sum of money, he will often fritter the money away on prolonged drinking sessions, because there are no financial advisors to guide him.

In September 2002, MDC leader Tsvangirai spoke to 25,000 of his supporters in Rufaro Stadium and is alleged to have said, "We say to Robert Mugabe, if you don't want to go peacefully, we will remove you violently."[8] This statement would have grave repercussions for Tsvangirai at a later date.

There were then an estimated 50,000 illegal immigrants in Zimbabwe, which begs the question, "Were conditions really worse in other countries?" The answer is "yes," at least as far as Angola and the Democratic Republic of Congo are concerned since these countries have for years been torn apart by civil strife. But there were also large numbers of immigrants from Mozambique, Zambia, and Malawi.

According to Chief Immigration Officer Elasto Mugwadi, no less than 1,653 people were granted permits for temporary employment, studency and scholarship in 2001–2002. Most of those who received permits came from China, South Africa, Britain (surprisingly enough!), Zambia, Malawi, the Congo, India, the United States, Angola, Canada and Kenya. A purge on the illegal immigrants was intended but was delayed, according to Mugwadi, as the government "did not want to draw unnecessary attention." Over that period, 299 people were given full residence permits.

What Mugwadi failed to make clear was that these individuals would undoubtedly have had to declare their loyalty to ZANU-PF. In fact, a cynic might say that, by allowing this immigration, Mugabe was playing a numbers game—replacing MDC supporters dying of starvation in Matabeleland with new immigrant recruits to ZANU-PF.[9]

In October 2002, Mugabe openly began to use his police force to impose his will on the white farmers, instead of leaving it solely to the war veterans as he had done before. After months of indifference to the harassment of these farmers, the police started to play an active role, arriving on the farms and manhandling their occupants. People such as Jimmy and Ruth Chatham, both 76, who sustained injuries to their arms when they were handcuffed, were told by the police that their papers (legal documents of ownership) meant nothing to them, and they were ordered to pack their bags. The police evicted 51 farmers from the Matabeleland region in the space of one week.

David Olds, whose mother Gloria and brother Martin were allegedly killed by war veterans, was threatened with arrest if he remained on his farm—even though no eviction order had been served on him. Some were given only five minutes to vacate their farms. Ernest Rosenfels of Marula, however, was arrested and released on bail of Z$4,000.[10]

On October 9, 2002, Mugabe told a visiting Afro-American delegation that Zimbabwe could not allow the Commonwealth to dictate terms that would not help the country to consolidate its right to self-determination. "The Commonwealth thinks it is an organisation like the United Nations," he said, whereas in fact it was a "loose club where we get associated with countries that were ruled by the former colonial power, Britain."

Sanctions had created pressures within the economy, but Mugabe felt the greatest chance for Zimbabwe's success lay in agriculture. "Without agriculture," he said, "our manufacturing sector collapses." He also explained that he had scrapped dual citizenship, because some whites had abused this facility. What shape this "abuse" took was not made clear.[11]

On October 13, 2002, Sir Garfield Todd (who had received a knighthood in 1989) died in hospital in Bulawayo, aged 94. His government of 1958 was credited with having made the first serious attempt to improve the education of blacks, when the number of black primary schools was increased from 20 in 1953 to 46 in 1960. Originally a supporter of the Mugabe government, Todd became disillusioned after the Matabeleland slaughter of 1983 and 1984. Nevertheless, after his retirement, he had donated 3,000 acres of his farmland to guerrillas disabled in the war for Independence. Mugabe had been a primary schoolteacher in Todd's New Zealand Churches of Christ

Mission School, and he recalled how he had once borrowed a book from Todd's wife, Grace.[12]

On October 17, 2002, U.N. officials confirmed that Mugabe had banned the charities Oxfam and Save the Children Fund from distributing food aid in the country.[13]

Innocent Gonese, the MDC's chief whip, attempted to present a petition to the Speaker of Zimbabwe's Parliament. It read, "We are disgusted that, of late, the unlawful arrests and torture have been directed at elected honourable Members of Parliament, who have been abused, ill-treated, and tortured by state agents...." The Speaker complained that Gonese was in breach of parliamentary procedure, because he should have presented the petition at the beginning of the session at 2:15 P.M. and not, as he had done, at 3:45 P.M. Gonese was ordered to sit down: he refused and was escorted out of the chamber, whereupon some 30 of his MDC parliamentary colleagues walked out.

There were precedents for this MDC boycott of Parliament, as in 2001, at an address by Joseph Kabila, president of the Democratic Republic of Congo, when the MDC argued that Kabila was not democratically elected; and at an address by President Mugabe, whom the MDC said it did not recognize as the head of state.[14]

On November 4, 2002, Chengetai Zvauya of Zimbabwe's independent Sunday newspaper *The Standard*, reported that the South African company Sasol had ceased supplying Zimbabwe with fuel.[15] On the same day, Sydney Masanvu, political editor of Zimbabwe's *Financial Gazette*, reported on the recent Insiza ballot. True to form, ZANU-PF had secured victory (by 12,115 votes to the MDC'S 5,102) by "violence, intimidation and the politicisation of food aid." The children of MDC supporters, in particular, had been prevented from receiving food, something that "defenceless and starving rural voters" were unable to withstand. By then the total number of political murders for 2002 had risen to 54: more than for the whole of 2001.[16]

A week before the Insiza Election, ZANU-PF seized food aid being distributed by the United Nations World Food Program, thereby denying it to "villagers suspected of supporting the MDC." MDC food aid intended for the starving was still being held up at Beitbridge on the border with South Africa, several months after it had arrived there.

According to Masanvu, unemployment was estimated at over 70 percent, with abject poverty afflicting nearly 80 percent of the population (compared with about 40–50 percent at Independence). Food production was down by over 60 percent compared with the previous season and close to seven million Zimbabweans—or half the population—faced starvation. Following the Insiza vote, ZANU-PF had increased its seats in the 150-member Parliament from 62 to 64, while the number of MDC seats had shrunk from 57 to 54. One analyst, who preferred not to be named, said, "The political playing field is too uneven for the MDC to compete effectively."

Those who criticize South Africa for not doing more to curb Mugabe's excesses may be unaware that that country's white farmers are having their own problems. In the area around the town of Lichtenburg, 100 miles west of Johannesburg, dozens of farmers have been murdered since the end of white rule, and the total number of murdered farmers for the country now stands at over 1,000. The head of the local farmers' union, Agri North West, is Willie Auret. "People break into farms when the owners go on Sunday to church," he stated, "and lie in wait. When the families come back they [the intruders] shoot them [the farmers] at point-blank range, rape the women, and mutilate the bodies." Auret explains how, for many of the whites, "a black is not even a human being": "If you are born with that sort of racism in you, it is not going to change overnight." The white Afrikaner community feels "threatened and vengeful."[17]

On November 13, 2002, an American university lecturer was murdered in Zimbabwe. Having been stopped at a roadblock and questioned about his papers, he had driven 12 miles to fetch his passport. Then, when he returned, he was shot and killed for no apparent reason.

A week later, members of an aid mission, which included an employee of the American embassy in Harare and an official of the United Nations, were beaten by Mugabe's war veterans. They were studying how to assist former farmworkers who had been displaced by the land seizures and who survived on a diet of berries and termites. The aid workers' "crime" was to throw food from their moving vehicle to these farmworkers.

Information Minister Jonathan Moyo was quick to explain the

reason for these beatings. They were the result of "interventionist behaviour by some U.S. embassy personnel who have been trespassing on to some farms under the guise of looking for alleged displaced farmworkers." In fact there were "no displaced farmworkers in Zimbabwe," said Moyo, "and the embassy knows that." Everyone knew that the United States was the "citadel of mafia conduct and racist vigilante groups," he said. "When will America restore its rule of law by controlling the mafia and the Klu Klux Klan?" Moyo dismissed the charge of lawlessness in Zimbabwe as being "quite preposterous."[18]

In December 2002, ZANU-PF held its annual congress in the small town of Chinhoyi in the north of the country—once Zimbabwe's biggest grain-producing area—which had become a wasteland of weeds. There, Mugabe, attired in a baseball cap bearing the slogan "Chave Chimurenga" ("It is now war"), addressed 2,000 people. "Leave us alone to run our affairs," he said. "We don't interfere in the affairs of Britain, and no one should interfere in our affairs." As usual, his speech contained much rhetoric and little substance. He did not specify exactly how Britain interfered in the affairs of Zimbabwe, but instead declared that if Britain's allies also wanted to interfere in Zimbabwe's governance, then "we will recognise them as enemies, like we recognise Britain, under Mr. Blair, as an enemy of Zimbabwe."[19]

"The more [western countries] work against us" and "the more they express their hostility," Mugabe declared, then "the more negative we shall become to their kith and kin here." Then his tone became more ominous and his language even more extreme. "We saw the British monster. It reared its head in an overt way. We will not rest until the serpent is dead. This monster also has the ability to breathe its spirit amongst us. We must send them [presumably the British] into the sea and see them drown." Imperialism, he said, was a two-headed monster: "When one head is crushed, the other stays alive."

There was no mention in his speech of the current food shortages or high inflation. Nevertheless, ZANU-PF's information secretary quickly dispelled any hope that the 78-year-old Mugabe might retire from office. "Who will want to retire," he inquired, "when we are faced with all these challenges?"[20]

Meanwhile, beef became the latest commodity to disappear from the shelves of Harare supermarkets; the local cattle farmers had been forced to slaughter their cattle when squatters set fire to the fields where the cattle had grazed. As Mugabe blamed food shortages on a drought earlier in the year, the World Food Program declared that at least 6.7 million Zimbabweans would require emergency food aid in the coming months.[21]

Mugabe's response to the growing fuel crisis was to accuse the Zimbabwean subsidiaries of Mobil, Caltex and BP of making excessive profits. "There has to be quick action," he said. "We do not want the holiday mood disturbed." The government could acquire these foreign-owned gas stations and distribute the fuel itself. His offer of compensation, however, was viewed with skepticism—similar offers had been made to the white farmers whose lands were nationalized, but, as far as is known, no money was ever actually paid out to them. Also, if Mugabe were to take over, could he oversee such as important commodity without the usual inefficiency and corruption?[22]

By late December 2002, motorists havd to queue for hours for gas, whilst public transport was paralyzed from the lack of fuel. This was because Zimbabwe was no longer able to fulfill the terms of the commodities-for-oil barter deal with Libya; Zimbabwe could not supply that country with beef, sugar and tobacco and, therefore, could not uphold its part of the bargain.[23]

No such fuel problems arise, however, for the presidential motorcade, which consists of two pairs of motorcyle outriders at the front and two armored cars equipped with machine guns at the rear of Mugabe's bullet-proof, stretch Mercedes limousine with its dark-tinted windows. Also included in the motorcade were vehicles belonging to his henchmen or other dignitaries and an ambulance. The motorcade travels at high speed—preferring roundabout routes rather than town centers—and zooms over bridges specially constructed above railway lines. Road traffic regulations state that when the motorcade (irreverently known as "Bob and the Wailers" because of the wailing sirens of the escort vehicles) passes by, it is a crime for anyone to "make any gesture or statement" within its "view or hearing ... with the intention of insulting any person travelling with an escort or any member of the escort." This was to prevent MDC supporters, some of whom had been arrested, from chanting the party's slogan "Chinja!" ("Change!") and from making the MDC's open-handed salute. The regulations also state that "the driver of every vehicle on the road on which a state motorcade is travelling ... shall halt his vehicle."[24]

The mismanagement of acquired farms and mistreatment of farmers is one thing; there then occurred a wave of mindless destruction and cruelty against livestock. On the Forrester Estates, 60 miles north of Harare, farmworkers, encouraged by government supporters, drove cattle into a dam, where all the terrifed animals drowned within an hour. Other cattle were locked in pens where, because of the searing heat, dehydration and food deprivation, they died slowly.

By the end of 2002, of the original 4,500 commercial farmers, fewer than 600 remained.[25] The survivors were tolerated only because they provided milk, cream, vegetables and meat to the ruling party, which, in their absence, would be starving like the rest of the population. On these labor-intensive farms (with their own schools and medical surgeries) were large communities of well-fed, well-educated, well-cared-for blacks, many of whom owned motorcycles and mobile telephones and played for the farm's football teams. How long could they survive?

When, in January 2002, Mugabe abolished dual nationality, 40,000 British people in Zimbabwe opted to retain their British passports: only a few thousand, mainly from the younger generation, opted for a Zimbabwean passport. However, although these 40,000, of whom about 20,000 are pensioners, were technically no longer Zimbabwean citizens, and although Mugabe was anxious to see them leave the country, the price of an airplane ticket to London had by then reached the colossal sum of Z$1 million. This was beyond most people's means.

13

Cricket and Coercion

Zimbabwe was brought into the spotlight when cricket's governing body, the International Cricket Council (ICC), decreed that six matches of the Cricket World Cup (of which Zimbabwe and South Africa were co-hosts) would be played in Harare and Bulawayo in February 2003. The chief executive of the ICC declared that his organization "did not make political judgments"; the England and Wales Cricket Board (ECB) lent their support to the ICC on the grounds that they themselves were "not a political organisation and do not make decisions on that basis." Downing Street agreed that this was a decision for the ICC, not for politicians.[1]

Clare Short, secretary of state for international development, took a very different view and described the decision to stage the matches in Zimbabwe as "deplorable and shocking." Nasser Hussain, the England team's captain, demanded that the government take responsibility for the decision on whether or not he should "lead the England team to Zimbabwe and perhaps shake the president [Mugabe] by the hand."[2] Peter Oborne, political correspondent for *The Spectator*, described the Cup proposal as an obscenity, and Peter Hain, now Welsh Secretary, said that, if the Cricket World Cup went ahead, Mugabe would be handed a propaganda victory, just as Hitler had received with the Berlin Olympics of 1936.[3]

Only a roadway separates Mugabe's presidential residence from

153

the Harare Sports Club and cricket ground where England and Zimbabwe would meet on February 13. The security arrangements for the match were to be handled by the Central Intelligence Organization, which, in the words of Roy Bennett, a farmer and MP for the MDC, was "a terror machine that takes its orders directly from Mugabe," and which had "spearheaded the campaign of rape, torture and killings."[4]

Mugabe, a patron of the Zimbabwe Cricket Union, stated in 1984 that "cricket civilises people and creates good gentlemen. I want everyone to learn cricket in Zimbabwe. I want ours to be a nation of gentlemen."[5] It was at that time that the notorious 5th Brigade were "ethnically cleansing" (i.e., murdering) tens of thousands of Ndebele in Matabeleland.

On January 6, 2003, it was announced that Mugabe would appoint (unelected) governors for Harare and Bulawayo. (Other towns and provinces already had governors appointed by Mugabe, all of whom were members of ZANU-PF.) This, in the words of MDC Local Government Minister Ignatius Chomboa, would make the mayors of those two cities "redundant," or at any rate it would "frustrate their work." The last vestige of democracy would be abolished.[6]

Pius Ncube, the 56-year-old Archbishop of St. Mary's Catholic Cathedral in Bulawayo, which had a congregation of 150,000 Ndebele, was not afraid to speak out. "People feel threatened and hounded by an evil regime," he said, "and it is important for people in positions like mine not to be silenced." The problem of starvation was worsning every day. Only the previous week, the archbishop had heard of a farmer who had not eaten for six days, but who still took his animals out to look for pastures to graze. "They found his body where he had gone to sleep," said the archbishop. "He was too weak to survive."[7]

In South Africa, where a "willing buyer, willing seller" scheme was in place, 80 percent of commercial farmland remained in the hands of whites. That country's labor minister, Membathisi Mdladlana, recognized this inequality. However, in view of the catastrophe in Zimbabwe, Mdladlana, adopting a more enlightened and practical approach than Mugabe, declared that black farmers should be resettled on farms only if they could produce commercial amounts of food.[8]

By January 2003, the amount of grain reaching Zimbabwe from South Africa had been reduced to a trickle, due to the lack of foreign currency required to pay for it. This situation was exacerbated by the Mugabe regime's refusal to allow the private importation of corn, a commodity in which the government had a trading monopoly.[9]

E-mails received from Zimbabwe in late December 2002 stated that the only items to be found on the shelves of its supermarkets were rolls of toilet paper; diesel fuel was nowhere to be found, and Harare was the only place where gasoline might be obtained—and this only in limited amounts. Even clean water was unobtainable in Harare, because there was no foreign currency with which to purchase the chemicals required for its sterilization. Christmas shoppers found that ATMs were unable to dispense money, since there was no foreign currency to pay for the import of the special paper on which the bank notes were printed.

On January 12, 2003, Peter Oborne of *The Spectator* described a recent visit he had made to Zimbabwe: he had entered the country posing as a golfer, but in reality had traveled widely, making secret films and recordings. He discovered an all-too-familiar situation: lorries laden with maize (from South Africa), which were transported under state monopoly control to the mills for the maize to be ground into mealie meal. ZANU-PF controlled the distribution of the mealie meal: it was only for their own supporters. The MDC's supporters were reduced to scavenging for roots and nuts, and they were even trying to eat the leaves from the trees. Some had tasted nothing but water for several days, yet 132 tons of MDC maize sat in a warehouse, because it had been impounded and it was rotting. Oborne described this as a pre-famine stage, where rural people were obliged to sell their cattle—their livelihood—in exchange for mealie meal. This was not entirely accurate, because for some it was too late; they were already dead.

The haunting images of Oborne's tragic film documentary stick in the mind. "Look how thin I have become!" says a black woman as she unbuttons her blouse to reveal her skeletal ribs. "We have no mealie meal, no sugar," says a black man weakly. "Nothing, everything; everything, nothing," says another man, despairingly. Their crime? To exercise their democratic right to vote for the opposition MDC Party and to be friendly toward white people. Their punishment? To suffer death by starvation.

The defeat of Kenya's President Daniel arap Moi (whose KANU Party had been in power in Kenya since 1963) in the elections of December 27, 2002, left the 78-year-old Mugabe as the only surviving head of state of his era. The question was did Mugabe himself contemplate retirement? In what appeared to be a tiny glimmer of hope, Morgan Tsvangirai, leader of the MDC, revealed that in December 2002 he had received a message from General Vitalis Zvinavashe, commander of the defense forces, and Emmerson Mnangagwa, Speaker of Parliament (who is seen as Mugabe's natural successor), asking for his views on the way forward, since Mugabe "had long indicated that he wanted to retire." Tsvangirai's reply was that he was "prepared to assist in the necessary transitional arrangements," but he made it "categorically clear" that this did not mean he would participate "in the formation of a government of national unity or some underhand pact with ZANU-PF." "We will never be party to any political arrangement that seeks to sanitise Mugabe's violent illegitimacy," said Tsvangirai.[10]

However, on January 14, Mugabe stated that he would "never, never, never" go into exile. He had fought for Zimbabwe, and when he died he would be buried in Zimbabwe. These false reports, he said, had been inspired by the British government. "I am not used to answering questions about nightmares which are dreamt at No. 10 Downing Street," he said.[11]

On January 15, the day after ECB Chief Executive Tim Lamb confirmed that England would indeed be going to Zimbabwe for the Cricket World Cup, Tsvangirai described Zimbabwe's economy as Mugabe's "greatest nemesis ... which refuses to bend to all his dictatorial formulae." "He cannot rig it, he cannot shoot it, he cannot intimidate it, and although he raped it, the economy continues to land fatal blows that Mugabe cannot block."[12]

On that same day, Tim Lamb explained why his cricket board had ignored political pressure for his team not to play in Zimbabwe, pointing out that (a) Britain still retained diplomatic relations with Zimbabwe; (b) no decision had been made to expel Zimbabwe from the Commonwealth; (c) 300 or more British companies still traded with Zimbabwe, and (d) British Airways still ran flights to Harare.

When Loveness Mangete, a teenager, attended mass at the

Church of St. Francis Xavier at Empandeni, west of Bulawayo, he made this pitiful statement: "It is not just that we do not have any food in our homes or in our fields. But even if we have any money we cannot buy any food because the shops do not have anything, so what can we do? Perhaps the only thing is to pray." Mugabe was baptized a Catholic, and he studied at the mission school at Empandeni after World War II. However, Archbishop Ncube described Mugabe's catholicity as "meaningless" and "bogus." "Love your neighbour as yourself," said the archbishop, was "one of the fundamental tenets," yet he did not see Mugabe "practising that principle," as he inflicted suffering on an entire nation.[13]

On January 19, it was reported that two of Mugabe's nephews, the sons of his older sister Sabina, had seized former white-owned farms, situated in Mugabe's home district of Zvimba, from the so-called war veterans. (Earlier in the month, these veterans had led major food riots in Harare and Bulawayo, demonstrating that even Mugabe's keenest supporters were turning against him.) Reacting bitterly to this event, Juliet Govha, leader of the war veterans in that area, complained that Mugabe's nephews had played no part in the "fight for land" and had only come "to reap where others have sown." "It's like thieves falling out," said a displaced white farmer.[14] At last, it was beginning to dawn on the war veterans that they had been duped, used by Mugabe merely as stepping-stones on his path to self-aggrandizement.

Meanwhile the *Times* revealed that Mugabe had recently returned home from a "lavish Christmas holiday in Thailand, Singapore and Malaysia." This despite the fact that the state-owned airline Air Zimbabwe was £18 million in debt. On the flight back to South Africa, ten seats were taken up by his wife, children, and other "camp followers," and no less than 15 trolleys, "piled high with packages labelled—State House, Harare—were loaded on board the aircraft."[15] Meanwhile, the Johannesburg *Sunday Times* reported that Information Minister Jonathan Moyo had recently visited Johannesburg, stayed at an expensive hotel, and bought luxury goods with a large amount of foreign currency.[16]

On January 24, 2003, the (British government–sponsored) Department for International Development in Harare stated that none of the £40 million of aid provided by the United Kingdom to

Zimbabwe in the year ending March 2003 "goes through the Government of Zimbabwe ... we instead work with NGOs [non-governmental organizations], the U.N. system and the private sector. A fundamental principle of our programme is that all food aid should be apolitical; we have detailed monitoring mechanisms in place to ensure programmes reach their intended beneficiaries."[17] Laudable as this statement may be, it bears little relationship to the situation on the ground, as witnessed by Peter Oborne and other impartial observers.

MDC Spokesman Paul Thembe Nyathi put it succinctly: "This is all about keeping Robert Mugabe in power. This is all about coercing the people of Zimbabwe to support a one-party mentality." Mugabe "had not divested himself of this mentality." He had been "dragged, kicking and screaming into a multi-party Culture—something he does not believe in. Now he has found a way of achieving a one-party state—by using food as a weapon. Then the rest of the international community has no one to deal with except Mugabe."[18]

On February 5, 2003, Morgan Tsvangirai, together with MDC Secretary Welshman Ncube and M.P. Renson Gasela, went on trial in Harare, charged under the Law and Order (Maintenance) Act. This Act was originally passed by the British colonial government in 1960, and it was the same law under which Mugabe was imprisoned for ten years. Under the Act, anything likely to "further or encourage" the violent ousting of the government constituted an "act of terrorism" and was punishable by life imprisonment.

The scene was described on a BBC program, "The World Tonight," by Andrew Meldrum of the *Guardian*. Present outside the courtroom were several hundred people, including diplomats from the European Union and other countries, lawyers, members of Parliament and journalists. They were denied access, however, by riot police armed with batons, tear gas and handguns. MDC supporters shouted "Chinja!" and "The government is rotten." They waved their outstretched hands in the characteristic MDC salute, and they also waved red cards, such as are used by football referees to dismiss an offender from the field of play. Two journalists, one a senior reporter from the country's only independent daily newspaper, the *Daily News*, and the other a freelance reporter, were arrested. Several of the E.U. diplomats made their way to the Department of Foreign Affairs to lodge an official protest.[19]

Paddington Garwe of the High Court intervened and directed that it was an open case, and, therefore, "members of the public and other interested persons" were to be admitted. The result was that the British high commissioner and the German and Spanish ambassadors were permitted to attend the afternoon session. The police refused to allow several journalists to enter, saying that the courtroom was filled to capacity, but lawyers inside stated that the public galleries were almost empty.[20]

The background of the case was that, in September 2002, Tsvangirai had made a speech in Harare, stating that if Mugabe did not go peacefully, then he would be removed "violently." The crime of the three who were accused was, according to Bharat Patel (the deputy attorney general who opened the case for the state), their desire "to overthrow a government and to occupy positions through undemocratic means." There had also been a meeting between Tsvangirai and one Ari Ben Menashe, who was the state's principal witness.

Menashe claimed to have previously been an arms dealer and to have also worked with the Israeli intelligence agency, Mossad. Menashe was currently head of a Canadian consulting firm called Dickens and Madson. However, it was on record that his firm had been hired by the Mugabe government in order to improve its image.

Tsvangirai claimed that the firm had offered to help the MDC improve its image in the West. Menashe, however, claimed that Tsvangirai "wanted him [Menashe] to have Mr. Mugabe killed." According to Tsvangirai, the audiotapes and videotapes of this meeting (which were presumably made without Tsvangirai's knowledge or consent) "show other people around him [Tsvangirai] making suggestive comments, but they do not show him actually discussing that [subject], affirming it, and it certainly does not show him ordering it [Mugabe's elimination]."[21] It was observed that the videotapes did not run in sequence, and George Bizos, the South African lawyer who led Tsvangirai's defense, stated that the government's evidence had been "heavily doctored," to implicate the three defendants.

It was significant that the government stopped short of ordering the imprisonment of Tsvangirai, either before or during his trial.

According to the *Guardian*'s Andrew Meldrum, this was because it was "apparently afraid to put him [Tsvangirai] in jail," as he was an extremely popular man in Harare. They were "going to have to deal with this very very carefully," because tensions were high.

At the one-hour hearing, Tsvangirai's lawyer, Chris Anderson, argued that Sections 51 and 58 of the Act under which his client was charged were unconstitutional. Presiding judge Moses Chinhengo agreed, and the case was referred to the Supreme Court. If Sections 51 and 58 were found to be consistent with the Constitution, the trial would resume. If not, Tsvangirai could still face a common-law charge of incitement to violence.[22]

Why was the trial held at that particular time? After all, only eight days later, the Cricket World Cup was due to begin in Zimbabwe, and the world's attention was firmly focused on that country but, as far as Mugabe was concerned, for quite the wrong reasons. It seems that the real purpose of the trial was to prevent Tsvangirai and his colleagues from participating in the forthcoming presidential elections, which were due in two months' time.

The same day, British Shadow Foreign Secretary Michael Ancram referred in a letter to the *Daily Telegraph* to French President Chirac's invitation to Mugabe to attend the Franco-African summit meeting in Paris on February 18 (the day after E.U. sanctions against Zimbabwe were due to expire). In Ancram's view, it would be a mistake for France to go ahead and greet Mugabe, because this would "grant him the legitimacy [that] he longs for." Clearly, the same would apply if Cricket World Cup matches were to be held in Zimbabwe.[23]

On February 10, 2003, at the Harare Sports Club, Andy Flower went in to bat for Zimbabwe in their Cricket World Cup match against Namibia. Flower, 34, was a white former Zimbabwean captain, who had topped the world Test Match batting averages in 2001. On his right sleeve, he wore a black armband, as did his fellow teammate Henry Olonga, who appeared on the pitch that afternoon, when it was Zimbabwe's turn to field. Olonga, 26, a fast bowler, was the first black Zimbabwean to represent his country.

The explanation for their armbands appeared in a joint statement, which they issued as the match started. In it, they said they were "deeply distressed about what is taking place in Zimbabwe in the midst of the World Cup." Therefore, they did not feel that they could take the field without indicating their feelings "in a dignified manner and in keeping with the spirit of cricket." They could not ignore the fact that millions of their compatriots were starved, unemployed and oppressed.

Flower and Olonga were aware that hundreds of thousands of Zimbabweans could die in the coming months through a combination of starvation, poverty and AIDS. Also, they knew that many people had been unjustly imprisoned and tortured simply for expressing their opinions about what was happening in the country. They had heard a torrent of racist hate directed at minority groups. They were aware that thousands of Zimbabweans were routinely denied their right to freedom of expression: that people had been murdered, raped, beaten and had their homes destroyed because of their beliefs, and that many of those responsible had not been prosecuted. Flower and Olonga had decided that they would wear the black armbands "for the duration of the World Cup." In doing so, they were "mourning the death of democracy" in their "beloved country" and "making a silent plea to those responsible to stop the abuse of human rights in Zimbabwe." Anyone with the remotest knowledge of Mugabe and his regime understood that, by their courageous action, these two Zimbabwean cricketers were taking a huge risk, not only with their own safety, but also with that of their friends and loved ones.[24]

Late in the afternoon of February 11, 2003, the chief executive of the ICC made an announcement. "I wish to advise that today the ECB has notified the ICC that it will not play its match scheduled for Harare on February 13, 2003. The ECB has cited its continuing safety concerns for its players as its reason for not meeting that commitment. You will be aware that yesterday ICC through its President, and the United Cricket Board of South Africa through its President, gave a direction to the ECB to comply with the fixture and play the match in Zimbabwe. The ECB has indicated today that it does not believe that that direction is reasonable, and accordingly ICC has moved to cancel the match."

In response, Tim Lamb of the ECB had this to say: "ECB considers that the well-being of its players would be endangered if it were to compel them to fulfill the fixture in Zimbabwe on February 13.

Secondly, ECB considers that the present state of disorder in Zimbabwe dictates that the fixture should be relocated."[25]

These statements were made after the ICC and ECB had taken legal advice on such matters as possible fines and penalty points that England might have to incur as a result of the cancellation. Behind the scenes, however, emotions were running high amongst the England players, particularly the younger ones, who considered it most unfair that they were being asked to shoulder responsibility for a decision that should have been made months ago by others better equipped to do so. As for the older players, no one wished to be remembered as part of the team that went to Zimbabwe.

14

In Perspective:
The Phenomenon of Mugabe

In the mid-nineteenth century, the time of Dr. David Living-stone, the whites attempted with some success to evangelize the blacks of Rhodesia. Then the colonial era of white rule followed, epitomized by Cecil Rhodes.

By the turn of the twentieth century, the scramble for Africa by European powers had left Britain as the largest colonizer, controlling over a dozen countries, including Kenya, Uganda, Tanganyika, Northern and Southern Rhodesia, and Nyasaland, in addition to Cape Province and Natal. To Transvaal and the Orange Free State, the British granted internal self-government on a whites-only franchise.

When his government declared the UDI in November 1965, Ian Smith flew in the face of everything that was going on around him. A federation created by the United Nations between Eritrea and Ethiopia (previously a British Protectorate) in 1952 made these the first countries in Africa to achieve independence. When Harold Macmillan made his "wind of change" speech in January 1960, only one country in black Africa—Ghana—had gained its independence in 1957; by the end of that year Kenya had been joined by a dozen others, and by 1962 every African country north of Angola, Northern Rhodesia, Nyasaland and Mozambique had followed suit.

Closer to home, Uganda achieved independence in 1962, and Northern Rhodesia and Nyasaland in 1964. Therefore, for Southern Rhodesia the writing, as it were, was on the wall. Botswana, however, would not achieve independence (from Britain) until 1966, Guinea Bissau (from Portugal) in 1974, Mozambique and Angola (from Portugal) in 1975, and Namibia (from South Africa) in 1988. As for South Africa, it had declared itself a republic and left the Commonwealth in 1961, and it was not until 1994 that the first free, nonracial elections gave victory to the African National Congress (ANC), and Nelson Mandela (who had been charged with conspiring to overthrow the South African government and sentenced to life imprisonment 30 years previously in 1964) became the country's new president.

As Ian Smith rightly pointed out, these changes were not achieved without bloodshed, particularly in Algeria, Chad, Sudan, Ethiopia/Eritrea, and the Congo,[1] and often, instead of colonial rule being replaced by parliamentary democracy, a despot had come into power. In Uganda, Milton Obote, president from 1966 to 1971, was deposed in a coup led by Army Commander Idi Amin Dada, who violently supressed any opposition. Obote returned to power from 1980 to 1985 but was again deposed, by Lieutenant General Tito Okello; it was not until 1986 that a coalition government was formed in Uganda. Nigeria endured a civil war following the secession of the province of Biafra in 1967, and Ghana endured 30 years of military rule after Kwame Nkrumah was deposed as president in 1966. The struggle for liberation by FRELIMO in Mozambique lasted ten years: the country gained its independence in 1975, but it did not have a multiparty system until 1994.

Kenya was a one-party state from 1969 to 1991; Zambia's (Northern Rhodesia) United National Independence Party was the only legal party between 1972 and 1991; and Malawi (Nyasaland) was a one-party state until 1994. All these countries subsequently adopted a multiparty system. Tanganyika merged with Zanzibar in 1964 to become Tanzania and has had a multiparty system since 1992.

Traumatic as these events were, they in no way nullify the legitimacy of the aspirations of the inhabitants of these countries for a democratic system of "one man, one vote." However, having opened the door to the prospect of eventual black majority rule with the 1962 and 1965 Constitutions, Smith slammed the door shut firmly with the 1969 Constitution, which made it virtually impossible for blacks to increase their political representation. To this extent, Mugabe was proved right in his belief that no amount of dialogue would persuade the Smith regime to loosen its grip on power.

Independence for Southern Rhodesia, as for so many former colonies not only in Africa but throughout the world, has brought dictatorship: in this case in the form of Robert Mugabe—a man who is absolutely intolerant of any opposition. Witness the Matabeleland genocide of 1983, which forced Joshua Nkomo into exile; the intimidation of Edgar Tekere who, in 1990, contested the presidency and whose party, ZUM, simply faded away after the savage beating of its members by Mugabe's thugs; the hounding of the Reverend Sithole, who was accused of plotting to assassinate him; and the disenfranchisement of vast numbers of people in the 2002 elections, including 93-year-old former prime minister Garfield Todd. When discussing Mugabe, Lord Acton's phrase "power tends to corrupt, and absolute power corrupts absolutely," springs immediately to mind.

How can the phenomenon of Mugabe be adequately explained? He is a petulant person who, when he cannot have his own way, reveals the same behavioral pattern over and over again. The problem festers in his mind and, as it does, he plans his spiteful and vindictive revenge. The opposition must not merely be defeated; it must be hunted down and annihilated—no matter the consequences. He has no respect for the rule of law and must always win, even if this means moving the proverbial goalposts. He is prepared to take on the whole world rather than to compromise, which would mean a loss of face. In a landlocked country surrounded by other countries not unsympathetic to his point of view, he feels able to behave more or less as he chooses.

His childhood poverty, together with his father's abandonment and the loss of his two elder brothers, followed by the loss of the only two children he and his first wife ever had, may have left Mugabe with a lasting legacy of fear and insecurity. This may explain not only why he is unable to make close friendships, but also why he has an overwhelming desire to cling to power, even if by doing so he brings upon himself the opprobium of the world and the ruination of his country.

Mugabe's years of imprisonment may also have had an adverse

effect on him. Researchers Krestev, Prokipidis and Sycamnias speak of prisoners achieving "absolution of any personal sense of guilt or responsibility for offences against society by emphasising and concentrating on society's real or fancied offences against them." This applies to Mugabe in the sense that he shows no concern for the victims of his government-instigated thuggery, while he constantly blames the whites, MDC supporters and Britain for all his problems.[2]

Mugabe is a well-read man, with seven university degrees and eleven honorary degrees from six countries (including his own), and in his time he has been chairman of many of Africa's most prestigious organizations. Yet, knowing fully that the colonial era is long since dead and buried, he continues with his cynical attempt to indoctrinate the masses with anticolonial rhetoric. He possesses a masters degree in economics from the University of London, yet he seems not to have the remotest idea of how the country's economy should be run. He steadfastly refuses to allow Zimbabwe to fulfill its destiny or to allow its people to embrace a new age—of travel, of experiencing other cultures, of making new friends, and of benefiting from worldwide communication offered by the media, particularly the Internet, with its infinite possibilities for the dissemination of knowledge and social intercourse throughout every corner of the globe.

In the Rhodesia of the 1950s, it was as if the Afrikaners were still, in their own minds, fighting the Boer War against the British. Now, half a century later, it seems that Mugabe, despite his country having gained independence, still remains locked into the old colonial "black versus white" ideology, when the rest of the world has long since moved on.

Mugabe is highly selective in his rhetoric, focusing on what he perceives to be bad and ignoring what is good. His arguments are sterile, unconstructive, and redundant. They lead nowhere. The British are "bad" by definition—there is no recognition of the millions of pounds of aid that the British government, on behalf of its taxpayers, has provided to Zimbabwe since Independence, nor is any thanks given to the citizens of Britain, who have donated generously to the charitable organizations operating there. For example, in the year ending in March 2003, the United Kingdom committed £40 million to Zimbabwe, of which £29 million was for food, and £7 million for "non-food humanitarian assistance [to support agricultural recovery in communal areas and for health support in terms of nutrition monitoring and epidemic control]." The balance was to be spent on "programmes to prevent and mitigate the spread of HIV/AIDS in the country, where the adult infection rate is 35 percent."[3]

As Mugabe whips up hysteria against Britain in particular in an attempt to make that country the scapegoat for all his woes, as far as his own country, Zimbabwe, is concerned, Mugabe is guilty, time and again, of dissimulation. He pretends to embrace democracy by holding elections, but he goes to any lengths to prevent his opponents from voting; he says grain will be imported for the benefit of "our people," but everyone knows that he is referring only to ZANU-PF and its supporters; he says that "loyal citizens" will be permitted to pursue a farming career, but the truth is that there will soon be no white farmers left. He accuses "some countries" and "regional blocks" of manipulation and intimidation, whilst at the same time siphoning off aid for himself, for his relations, and for his henchmen. By describing the "black majority" as the "right holders" of the land, he reveals an inherently racist agenda. There is no attempt to compromise with the white farmers, to acknowledge that it is they who have the experience and expertise to feed the people, and that it would be in the general interest to seek their cooperation. And never does he show an inkling of remorse for the crimes committed in his name, against either black or white persons, not even for the appalling genocide that occurred in Matabeleland.

As for the MDC, it is a legitimate political organization whose followers have the same aspirations and capacity for suffering as everybody else; yet Mugabe stubbornly denies its followers basic human rights, even their right to life itself. His venom is not directed solely at whites, as black supporters of the MDC have had the initials of ZANU-PF carved into the skins of their backs by the knives of his agents.[4]

Ambition is undoubtedly a primary motivating factor in Mugabe's psyche, but his flamboyant baseball caps and psychedelic shirts (that make him seem relaxed and easygoing) may mask a variety of fears within him: fear that there will be a resurgence of white rule (however absurd this may seem), which will bring with it his return to prison to face further humiliation at the hands of white jail-ers; or fear that he will be deposed from power, and will regress into the state of being one who is controlled, rather than one who controls, so that the many enemies he has made since he came to power will then be in a position to call him to account for his many crimes against humanity.

15

Thoughts on Leadership and the Future

Today there is starvation in Zimbabwe, exacerbated by years of economic mismanagement and two years of drought, and applied selectively by Mugabe cynically to further his own ends. An image is often evoked of a fence, on one side of which are lush fields burgeoning with crops of tobacco and maize, while on the other lies a wasteland of weeds, clogged irrigation channels, broken pipes and rusting machinery. There are no prizes for guessing which is the "resettled" farm! Another unforgettable image is of people queuing for hours and sometimes days to vote, showing immense courage and knowing that they are risking their lives and those of their families if they choose any other party than ZANU-PF. Even if a child in an MDC area was fortunate enough to obtain a bowl of maize-based porridge at school, becoming an orphan was the best he or she could look forward to, as both parents would soon be dead from starvation.

In contrast to Mugabe, Nelson Mandela, who was imprisoned for 27 years and therefore had even more reason to be bitter, is revered throughout the world for his conciliatory demeanor and for his renunciation of violence.

As a young person Mugabe showed great promise; yet as a ruler he has failed to live up to the expectations of his fellow countrymen and women and in particular of the less well-off. He has shown nothing but hatred and vituperation to those impertinent enough to take any view that does not happen to coincide with his own. Behind his benign smile and plausible voice lies the heart of a remorseless and unrelenting man.

It is impossible to find a single virtue in Mugabe and his regime. This former mission schoolboy has broken most, if not all, of the ten commandments, some repeatedly, without any sign of remorse. The qualities of love, compassion, honor, justice, forgiveness, and fair play— characteristics that high-minded poets, writers and philosophers throughout the ages have agreed are virtues that ennoble and civilize mankind—appear to have been wholly dispensed with.

So who, if anyone, would come to the aid of the beleaguered black and white people of Zimbabwe? The United Nations? The United States? Either is an unlikely prospect, since both are presently preoccupied with the problem of global terrorism in general and of Iraq in particular. The European Union? Perhaps even more unlikely, since, according to Oborne, Belgium traditionally blocks any possibility of intervention because of its own agenda in the Congo. Tony Blair declared in a speech to his Labour Party Conference in 2001 that there would be "no toleration of bad governance, from the endemic corruption of some states, to the activities of Mr. Mugabe's henchmen in Zimbabwe," and that "if Ruanda happened again today, as it did in 1993 when a million people were slaughtered in cold blood ...," then "[Britain] would have a moral duty to act there also." And yet as far as taking any action is concerned, in the words of Peter Oborne, the British government, "with its famous ethical foreign policy," appears to be completely "paralysed."

Would the Zulus of South Africa hear the desperate cries of their distant relatives, the Ndebele of Zimbabwe, and persuade their leader Mbeki to tell Mugabe in no uncertain terms that enough is enough, he must curb his excesses, and show humanity instead of hatred? And yet it is not just they who suffer, for even Mugabe's own supporters now face ruination and starvation.

South African President Thabo Mbeki is, of all people, in the best position to bring Mugabe to heel. He has only to cut off the country's supplies of electricity, fuel oil and maize, and Zimbabwe would soon be on its knees. So why does he not act? When the deputy president of South Africa, Jacob Zuma, was recently asked a question in Parliament about Zimbabwe, his response was the following: "What is it in Zimbabwe that makes everyone so agitated? Let us deal with the matters without mentioning Zimbabwe. I don't think we want to enter into that debate."[1]

It is to be hoped that one day these nightmarish times will pass and that the final phase of Zimbabwe's evolution as a nation will bring a true and meaningful democracy in which all the people

Nelson Mandela (courtesy of the South African High Commission, London).

of the country have some influence in its government. In the words of Winston Churchill, "No one pretends that democracy is perfect or all-wise. Indeed, it has been said that democracy is the worst form of Government, except all those other forms that have been tried from time to time." And it is some consolation that even Mugabe cannot destroy the basic potential of the country—its rich land, its minerals, and of course its people.

Archbishop Desmond Tutu of South Africa—a two-time winner of the Nobel Peace Prize—who as archbishop of Cape Town struggled against apartheid, was himself traumatized by the harrowing stories he heard recounted by witnesses at his Truth and Reconciliation Commission; one of the purposes of this commission, he stated, was to help heal a wounded people. Perhaps he should have the last

171

word here. "Our experiment is going to succeed because God wants us to succeed, not for our glory and aggrandisement but for the sake of God's world. God wants to show that there is life after conflict and repression—that because of forgiveness, there is a future."[2]

16

Recent Developments

On February 19, 2003, Henry Olonga was expelled from the Takushinga Cricket Club of Harare and dropped from the national team for daring to protest against the Mugabe regime by wearing a black armband. That same day, Amnesty International called on Zimbabwe's neighbors to end the "cycle of repression, arrests, and torture inflicted upon those who peacefully express their opinions and who do not share the government's view." Meanwhile, the Amani Trust (an organization similar to the Runnymede Trust, which Sally Mugabe had once worked for) stated that more than 1,000 people had been tortured in the previous year, mainly by police detectives, without any of the perpetrators being brought to trial.

On February 20, 2003, Mugabe arrived in Paris to attend the Franco-African Summit, in a week when the European Union renewed sanctions (including a travel ban on Mugabe) against Zimbabwe. While he was selectively starving his people, Mugabe enjoyed the hospitality of the Hotel Plaza Athénée, where his entourage occupied no fewer than 33 rooms; he and his wife resided in the presidential suite, at a cost of £2,850 per day. Peter Tatchell traveled to Paris in the hopes of persuading a French court to order the arrest of Mugabe on charges of torture, but he was unsuccessful.

Meanwhile, Ari Ben Menashe, the prosecution's witness in the trial of Morgan Tsvangirai, admitted under cross-examination that he and his colleagues had tricked Tsvangirai in order to tape-record incriminating evidence against him.

Damning evidence came to light regarding vote-rigging in the presidential election in March 2002, when Mugabe defeated Tsvangirai by 434,000 votes. According to Registrar-General Tobaiwa Mudende, the electoral role for Zimbabwe in January 2002 contained 5.2 million names (this was later increased to 5.6 million with the addition of illegal registrations from ZANU-PF strongholds). However, census records show that the adult population of Zimbabwe in August 2002 totaled only 4.7 million. Of these, probably not more than 80 percent had ever registered to vote: this meant that the number of votes cast in the election could not have exceeded 3.7 million. The only possible conclusion is that between 1.5 million and 1.9 million people (depending on which of Mudende's figures is correct) voted who did not actually exist. There must have been vote-rigging on a massive scale, and despite Mugabe having been given a unanimous vote of confidence by the Non-Aligned States in February 2003, this is proof, if anymore was needed, that he should not be regarded as the legitimate president of Zimbabwe.[1]

On March 5, 2003, at the ongoing trial of Tsvangirai, Ari Ben Menashe told the court that at his first and second meetings with Tsvangirai—both held in London—the latter had agreed to the assassination of President Mugabe, but, at their third meeting in Montreal in Canada, Tsvangirai had backtracked, having realized the seriousness of the matter. Menashe denied that he was in the employ of the Zimbabwean government. If this is the truth, what were Menashe's motives and what did he have to gain by his involvement with the MDC leader?[2]

On that same day, Anthony Bailey, in a letter to the *Times*, asked why, in view of his behavior, Mugabe had not been stripped of his Honorary Knight Grand Cross of the Most Honourable Order of the Bath, when there was already a precedent for this (i.e., the case of Romanian dictator Nicolae Ceauşescu).[3]

On March 7, 2003, President George W. Bush brought the United States into line with Europe by imposing economic sanctions on Mugabe and on 76 of his government officials. He froze their assets and barred Americans from dealings with them. "Over the course of more than two years," said Bush, "the government of Zimbabwe has systematically undermined that nation's democratic institutions, employing violence, intimidation, and repressive means, including legislation, to stifle opposition to its rule." In fact, Mugabe had been guilty of this, not for two years, but for over twenty years.[4]

All too often in the past, cruel dictators have brought mayhem and misery, not only to their neighbors, but also to their own people—dictators like Joseph Stalin (Russia), Adolf Hitler (Germany), Idi Amin (Uganda), Nicolae Ceauşescu (Romania), Augusto Pinochet (Chile) and Pol Pot (Cambodia) to name but a few. Of course, we cannot forget Robert Mugabe. In fact, dictatorship is a pattern of behavior that dates back to the time of the Roman emperors Nero and Caligula, if not to the very origins of humanity.

Today, however, for the first time there is hope that in the future such enemies of humanity may be brought to justice for their crimes. On March 11, 2003, the world's first permanent War Crimes Court swore in its first 18 judges in The Hague in the presence of United Nations Secretary-General Kofi Annan. It is to be hoped that the very existence of this court may give immoral leaders, such as Robert Mugabe, pause for thought.[5]

The question is how can such dictators be prevented from performing and continuing to perpetrate their evil misdeeds? On March 19, 2003, at the United Nations, Russian Foreign Minister Igor Ivanov expressed the view that previous U.N. resolutions on Iraq and Iraqi leader Saddam Hussein, were specifically focused on that country's disarmament, not on removing its president. France's foreign minister, Dominique de Villepin, said, "An outbreak of force in such an unstable area can only exacerbate the tensions and fractures on which terrorists feed." Germany's foreign minister, Joschka Fischer, said, "There is no basis in the U.N. charter for a regime change with military means."[6] On the proactive side for disarmament were the United States, Great Britain and Spain: a coalition headed by President George W. Bush, which gave Hussein until 1 A.M. on the morning of March 20 to flee Iraq (which he failed to do), or else face war.

In April 2003, Liberal Democrat peer Lord Watson proposed that Mugabe be stripped of his honorary knighthood, bestowed in 1994, because of deteriorating human rights in Zimbabwe.

Mugabe, who proclaims that Zimbabweans "are a people of simple needs," currently owns no less than four palatial residences, including a holiday home near Cape Town: also at least four farms, previously owned by whites. His latest creation is a mansion costing an estimated £3.75 million. It has twenty-five bedrooms, ceilings designed by Arabic craftsmen, and glazed blue roofing tiles imported from China. There are two lakes in its grounds.[5]

Meanwhile, as those who have recently visited Zimbabwe will testify, the manufacture and sale of coffins is one of the few—if not only—growth industry in this tragic land.

Leaders of 54 Commonwealth nations met in the Nigerian capital Abuja in December 2003. Among the topics under discussion was the question of whether Zimbabwe's suspension from that organization should be continued. In the event, the leaders decided that it should.

"This is unacceptable," Mugabe is quoted as saying on hearing the news. His government responded immediately with a statement saying that "Accordingly, Zimbabwe has withdrawn its membership from the Commonwealth with immediate effect."

Meanwhile, opposition leader Morgan Tsvangirai was due to appear in court for the continuation of his hearing on charges of treason dating back two years. This has become Zimbabwe's longest running criminal trial. Tsvangirai also faces a second charge, that of allegedly inciting his supporters in June 2003 to overthrow the government.

Four hundred years ago, Shakespeare's character Hamlet faced the same dilemma as the world now faces regarding Robert Mugabe—whether to use force or not—and Hamlet articulated it thus: "To be or not to be, that is the question, whether 'tis nobler in the mind to suffer the slings and arrows of outrageous fortune, or to take arms against a sea of trouble, and, by opposing, end them."

Notes

Chapter 1

1. E. Rosenthal, p. 39.
2. R. Oliver and J. D. Fage, p. 34.
3. *Ibid.*
4. *Ibid.*, p. 111.
5. V. Da Silva.
6. R. Hall, p. 21.
7. *Ibid.*
8. *Ibid.*, p. 22.
9. *Herald.*
10. *Ibid.*
11. V. Da Silva.
12. *Herald.*
13. V. Da Silva.
14. *Ibid.*
15. Middleton, p. 430.
16. *Ibid.*, p. 432.
17. Letter, Jeremy Coote, Head of Collections, Pitt Rivers Museum, Oxford, to Dr. A. Norman, July 18, 2002.

Chapter 2

1. D. Blair, p. 18.
2. D. Smith and C. Simpson, p. 15.
3. T. Royle, p. 214.

Chapter 3

1. M. Meredith, p. 24.
2. *Ibid.*, p. 26.
3. T. Royle, p. 231.
4. M. Meredith, p. 27.
5. I. D. Smith, p. 41.
6. 1961 Constitution.
7. M. Meredith, p. 31.
8. *Ibid.*

Chapter 4

1. D. Healey, p. 223.
2. *Ibid.*, p. 332.
3. D. Smith and C. Simpson, p. 56.
4. M. Meredith, p. 36.
5. T. Royle, p. 251.

Chapter 5

1. *The Rhodesia Herald* (Salisbury, Southern Rhodesia), January 27, 1976.
2. T. Royle, p. 259.
3. *The Observer*, October 10, 1976.
4. D. Smith and C. Simpson, p. 95.

5. *The Rhodesia Herald*, March 17, 1977.
6. D. Smith and C. Simpson, p. 101.
7. *Ibid.*, p. 113.
8. *Ibid.*, p. 119.

Chapter 6

1. D. Smith and C. Simpson, p. 130.
2. *Ibid.*, p. 141.
3. Lancaster House Agreement.
4. D. Smith and C. Simpson, p. 168.
5. *Ibid.*, p. 171.
6. *Ibid.*, p. 184.

Chapter 7

1. M. Meredith, p. 39.
2. *Ibid.*, p. 15.
3. D. Smith and C. Simpson, p. 213.
4. D. Blair, p. 14.
5. D. Smith and C. Simpson, p. 210.
6. M. Meredith, p. 41.
7. D. Blair, p. 16.
8. *Ibid.*, p. 133.
9. M. Meredith, p. 52.
10. *Ibid.*, p. 163.
11. D. Blair, p. 29.
12. M. Meredith, p. 96.
13. *Ibid.*, p. 86.

Chapter 8

1. J. House, *et al.*, p. 69.
2. D. Smith and C. Simpson, p. 217.
3. M. Meredith, p. 122.
4. *Ibid.*, p. 97.
5. *Ibid.*, p. 126.
6. *Ibid.*, p. 105.
7. *Ibid.*, p. 137.
8. D. Blair, p. 133.

9 M. Meredith, p. 137
10. *Ibid.*, p. 154.
11. *Ibid.*, p. 156.
12. *Ibid.*, p. 157.

Chapter 9

1. D. Blair, p. 59.
2. *Ibid.*, p. 75.
3. *Ibid.*, p. 76.
4. *Ibid.*, p. 138.

Chapter 10

1. *The Economist*, May 6–12, 2000.
2. *The Daily Telegraph*, March 6, 2002, Peta Thornycroft.
3. *Ibid.*
4. *The Sunday Times*, March 10, 2002, R. W. Johnson and Jacqui Goddard.
5. *Ibid.*, March 24, 2002, Jon Swain.
6. *Ibid.*
7. *Ibid.*
8. *The Daily Telegraph*, March 6, 2002, Ambrose Evans-Pritchard.
9. *The Economist*, March 16–22, 2002.
10. *Ibid.*, September 15–21, 2002.
11. *Ibid.*, March 2–8, 2002.
12. *The Times*, June 13, 2002, Michael Dynes.
13. *Ibid.*
14. *The Weekend Tribune* (published by Media Africa Group), October 5–6, 2002, Basil Sithole.

Chapter 11

1. *The Mail on Sunday*, July 14, 2002, Jane Laing.
2. *The Daily Telegraph*, June 22, 2002, Peta Thornycroft.
3. *The Sunday Times*, June 30, 2002, R. W. Johnson.

4. *Ibid.*

5. *The Financial Gazette*, June 13–19, 2002, Sydney Masamvu.

6. BBC 1, Ceefax.

7. *The Sunday Times*, August 18, 2002, Tom Walker, R. W. Johnson, Nicholas Rufford and David Leppard.

8. *The Economist*, July 20, 2002.

9. *The Times*, July 24, 2002, Jan Raath.

10. *The Sunday Telegraph*, July 28, 2002, Christina Lamb and David Bamber.

11. *The Daily Telegraph*, August 17, 2002, Neil Tweedie.

12. ZANU-PF home page, www.zampfpub.co.zw/campaign2002.html.

13. www.mdczimbabwe.com/archive mat/statements/general/mt020812hero txt.htm.

14. *The Daily Telegraph*, August 17, 2002, Peta Thornycroft.

15. *Ibid.*, August 24, 2002, Andrew Sparrow.

16. *Ibid.*, August 24, 2002, Tim Butcher.

17. Department for International Development (DFID), Harare, Zimbabwe, January 24, 2003.

18. *The Sunday Telegraph*, July 28, 2002, Christina Lamb.

19. *The Sunday Times*, August 11, 2002, R. W. Johnson and Jon Swain.

Chapter 12

1. www.zampfpub.co.zw/campaign 2002.html.

2. *The Sunday Times*, August 31, 2002, Jonathan Leake and David Cracknell.

3. *The Daily Telegraph*, September 2, 2002, Tim Butcher.

4. *The Sunday Times*, September 8, 2002, R. W. Johnson.

5. *The Daily News* (Harare, Zimbabwe), September 19, 2002, Saul Gwakuba Ndlovu.

6. *The Daily News*, September 25, 2002, Reuters.

7. *Ibid.*, September 30, 2002, Cathy Buckle.

8. *The Daily Telegraph*, February 10, 2003, David Blair.

9. *The Weekend Tribune*, September 21–22, 2002, Faith Zaba.

10. *The Daily News*, October 8, 2002, Sandra Mujokoro.

11. *The Herald* (Harare, Zimbabwe), October 10, 2002, *Herald* reporter.

12. Rhodesians Worldwide, October–December 2002, vol. 18, no. 2, Fred Bridgland.

13. *The Guardian Unlimited*.

14. *The Weekend Tribune*, October 5–6, 2002, Faith Zaba.

15. www.thestandard.co.zw. (Harare)

16. www.africaonline.com/site/Arti cles/1,3,50637.jsp.

17. *The Daily Telegraph*, November 16, 2002, Tim Butcher.

18. *The Guardian*, November 20, 2002, Andrew Meldrum.

19. *The Times*, December 14, 2002, Jan Raath.

20. *The Daily Telegraph*, December 14, 2002, Peta Thornycroft.

21. *The Times*, December 14, 2002, Jan Raath.

22. *The Daily Telegraph*, December 16, 2002, Tim Butcher.

23. *The Sunday Herald* (Harare), December 12, 2002, Cris Chinaka.

24. Rhodesians Worldwide, October–December 2002, vol. 18, no. 2.

25. *The Daily Telegraph*, December 17, 2002, Peta Thornycroft.

Chapter 13

1. *The Daily Telegraph*, December 28, 2002, Kate Hoey.

2. *The Sunday Telegraph*, December 29, 2002, Rajeev Syal and Francis Elliott.
3. *The Times*, January 6, 2003, David Charter.
4. *The Sunday Telegraph*, January 19, 2003, Philip Sherwell.
5. *Ibid.*
6. *The Independent*, January 7, 2003, Stella Mapenzauswa.
7. *The Daily Telegraph*, January 11, 2003, Tim Butcher.
8. *Ibid.*
9. *The Daily Telegraph*, January 8, 2003, Peta Thornycroft.
10. *The Times*, January 16, 2003, Jan Raath.
11. *Ibid.*, January 15, 2003, Jan Raath.
12. *Ibid.*, January 16, 2003, Jan Raath.
13. *The Daily Telegraph*, January 17, 2003, Tim Butcher.
14. *The Sunday Telegraph*, January 19, 2003, Philip Sherwell.
15. *The Times*, January 24, 2003, Philip Webster, Adam Sage and Rory Watson.
16. *The Daily Telegraph*, January 20, 2003, Christopher Munnion and Peta Thornycroft.
17. DFID, Harare, January 24, 2003.
18. "Mugabe's Secret Famine." Channel 4, January 12, 2003, directed by Paul Yule.
19. *BBC—The World Tonight*, February 3, 2003, Andrew Meldrum.
20. *The Guardian*, February 4, 2003, Andrew Meldrum.
21. *BBC—The World Tonight*, February 3, 2003, Andrew Meldrum.
22. *The Daily Telegraph*, February 10, 2003, David Blair.
23. Letter to *The Daily Telegraph*, February 4, 2003, Michael Ancram.
24. *The Times*, February 11, 2003, Owen Slot.
25. BBC News 24 at 6 p.m., February 11, 2003.

Chapter 14

1. I. D. Smith, pp. 107–108.
2. J. Krestev, *et al.*, June 22, 2002.
3. DFID, Harare, January 24, 2003.
4. *The Sunday Times*, March 3, 2002, R. W. Johnson and Jacqui Goddard.

Chapter 15

1. *The Sunday Times*, March 3, 2002, R. W. Johnson and Jacqui Goddard.
2. D. Tutu, p. 230.

Chapter 16

1. *The Sunday Times*, March 2, 2003, R. W. Johnson.
2. *The Herald Online*, March 6, 2003, court reporter.
3. *The Times*, March 5, 2003, Anthony Bailey.
4. *Ibid.*, March 8, 2003, Reuters.
5. BBC News, Television Centre, Wood Lane, London.
6. *The Independent*, March 20, 2003, David Usborne.
7. The Daily Telegraph, December 8, 2003, Anton La Guardia.
8. Zimbabwenews.com, December 2, 2003.

Bibliography

Blair, David. *Degrees in Violence*. London: Continuum, 2002.

Cary, Robert, and Diana Mitchell. *African Nationalist Leaders in Rhodesia, Who's Who*. Bulawayo: Books of Rhodesia, 1977.

Daily News. Harare, Zimbabwe.

The Daily Telegraph. 1 Canada Square, Canary Wharf, London.

Da Silva, Vicky. "The Land Issue in Zimbabwe." *EISA*. February 25, 2002.

DFID—Department for International Development, P.O. Box 1030, Harare, Zimbabwe.

The Economist. 25 St. James's Street, London.

Ferris, N. S. *Know Your Rhodesia and Nyasaland*. Bulawayo: The Rhodesian Printing and Publishing Company, Ltd., 1956.

The Financial Gazette. Harare.

The Guardian. 119 Farrington Road, London.

The Gwelo Times. Gwelo, Southern Rhodesia.

Hall, Richard. "White Rhodesians: How They Got There." *The Observer Magazine, Ltd.*, London. November 21, 1965.

Harris, Julie. "My Memories."

Healey, Denis. *The Time of My Life*. New York: W. W. Norton, 1990.

The Herald. Zimbabwe Newspapers Ltd., Herald House, George Silunkika Avenue, Harare.

The Herald Online (Harare). www.herald.co.zw.

HMSO. Now the Stationary Office Ltd., Norwich, U.K.

House, Margaret, John House, and Beryl Salt. *Zimbabwe: A Handbook*. Harare: Mercury Press (Pvt) Ltd., 1983.

The Independent, Independent House, 191 Marsh Wall, London.

Krestev, Jenny, Pathena Prokipidis, and Evan Sycamnias. "The Psychological Effects of Imprisonment." www.uplink.com.au/lawlibrary/Documents/Docs/Doc82.html. 2002.

La Guardia, Anton. *The Daily Telegraph.*

Mail on Sunday. Northcliffe House, Kensington, London.

Meredith, Martin. *Mugabe: Power and Plunder in Zimbabwe.* Oxford: Public Affairs, Ltd., 2002.

Middleton, John. *Encyclopaedia of Africa South of the Sahara.* New York: C. Scribner's Sons, 1997.

The Observer. 119 Farringdon Road, London.

Ogrizek, Doré. *South and Central Africa.* New York: McGraw-Hill, 1954.

Oliver, Roland, and J. D. Fage. *A Short History of Africa.* 6th ed. New York: Penguin Books, 1988.

Report of the Constitutional Conference, Lancaster House, London. September–December 1979.

The Rhodesia Herald. Salisbury, Southern Rhodesia.

Rhodesian Schools Exploration Society Report. Lower Sabi Expedition, September 1958.

Rhodesians Worldwide. P. O. Box 22034, Mesa, Arizona, United States.

Rosenthal, Eric. *Encyclopaedia of Southern Africa.* 6th ed. London: Frederick Warne & Co., Ltd., 1973.

Royle, Trevor. *Winds of Change: The End of Empire in Africa.* London: John Murray, 1996.

Smith, David, and C. Simpson, with Ian Davies. *Mugabe.* London: Sphere Books, Ltd., 1981.

Smith, Ian Douglas. *Bitter Harvest: The Great Betrayal.* London: Blake Publishing, Ltd., 2001.

Southern Rhodesian Constitution, London. June 1961.

The Standard. Harare.

The Sunday Herald. Harare.

The Sunday Times. 1 Pennington Street, London.

The Times. Times Newspapers, Ltd. 1 Virginia Street, London.

Tutu, Desmond. *No Future without Forgiveness.* London: Rider. 1999.

The Weekend Tribune. Media Africa Group. www.africaonline.com.

Whitaker's Almanac. London: A&C Black, Ltd.

ZANU-PF website (and presidential website). www.gta.gov.zw/President%20Bio/bio_main.htm

zimbabwenews.com

Index